A Definitive Guide to

Microsoft

Excel 2019

A Step by Step Guide to Master Microsoft Excel Formulas and Functions
for Accounting, Data Analysis and Business Modeling

DERRICK
RICHARD

Copyright

Contents

Why This Guide?

This book is intended for anyone looking to learn the basics of applying Excel's robust Data analysis and statistical tools to their businesses or work activities. If understanding statistics is a major challenge or you are not especially mathematically-inclined, or if you want a spreadsheet package to put your business or accounting needs together, then this is the right book for you.

Here you'll learn how to use key data analysis and statistical tests using Excel 2019 without being overwhelmed by the underlying theory. This book clearly and methodically shows and explains how to create and use Excel formulas and functions to solve practical problems in your business.

Excel 2019 is a readily available computer program for students, instructors, and business owners. It is also an effective teaching and learning tool for quantitative analyses in Accounting and business courses. Excel's powerful numerical computational ability and graphical functions make learning this package a necessity.

This practical guide shows Excel's capabilities and focuses on rendering the subject as simple as possible appropriately and efficiently.

Some of the unique features of this book include:
- A step by step guide on how to use Excel and a detailed explanation of each action so that you can understand how to apply them.
- Includes specific objectives for each Excel function and how to apply them.
- Includes over 120 screenshots to help you perform the Excel steps correctly
- The book contains practical examples and problems taken from business models.

- Functions and formulas are explained in clear and straightforward terms without bogging you down with mathematical details.
- This book will teach you how to create each Excel file used in the illustrations yourself. Note that you are expected to develop an Excel file for your business.
- This book will give you ample practical illustrations on how to develop your Excel files.
- Each section presents the steps needed to solve a practical business problem using Excel formulas and functions.
- Includes how to perform complex calculations, and create a database.
- This book will also teach you Excel features like Charts, Collaboration, Data Loss Protection, Smart Lookups, Text lines in a cell, Enhanced PivotTable, Multi-select Slicer, etc.
- A "List of Microsoft Excel Keyboard Shortcut Keys" is given in Appendix A.

This book is appropriate for Data Analysis, Business Modeling and Accounting. It also helps users who wish to understand the basics as well as advanced Excel Functions or improve their Excel skills.

Chapter One
Introduction

Opening Excel Worksheet

There are several ways to open the 2019 Microsoft Excel in Windows 10. First, click on the "Start button ⊞." The programs are sorted out alphabetically › scroll down to the programs that start with the alphabet "E" › Search for "Excel" and click on it to open up the Excel program.

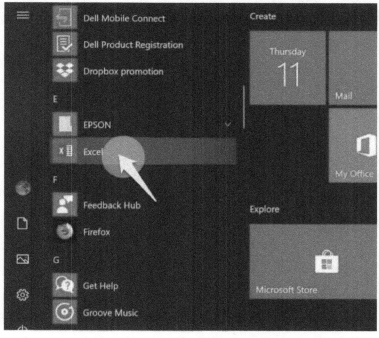

Alternatively, you can create a shortcut for the Excel program on the Desktop or the Taskbar for ease of access. To create a shortcut on the Desktop, left-click and drag the Excel icon on the start menu to the point on the Desktop, you wish to place it and let go when the "Link icon ⬀"pops-up. However, to open the Microsoft Excel program from its Desktop shortcut, Double-click on the Excel shortcut icon on the desktop. Alternatively, you can add the Excel program to the Taskbar, click on the start button > scroll down to "Excel" Right-click on it > click on "More" and "Pin to taskbar."

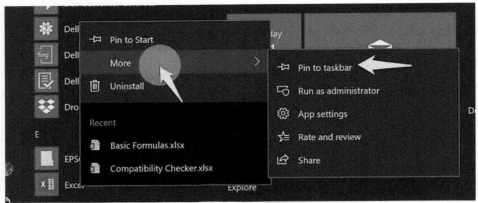

This places the Excel Program icon on the Taskbar. The Excel program is opened up from the Taskbar with a single click.

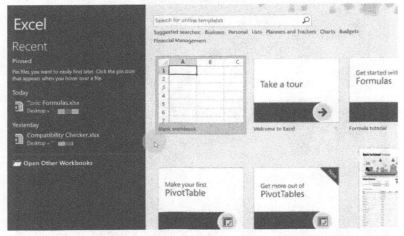

If you open up Excel 2019 for the first time, you will see that it is divided into two sections. On the left-hand side, you have the most recent programs you opened up and on the right, you have all the Excel templates and several offers that could aid your Excel journey. To start a blank Excel file, click on the "Blank Workbook" to get started. If

2

you want to search for a saved workbook that is not pinned to the side of the Recent file Window, click on "Open Other workbooks" and search for the workbook, you have saved and select "Open."

New Workbook

Whenever you open Excel and click on the "Blank Workbook," the image below is what you see.

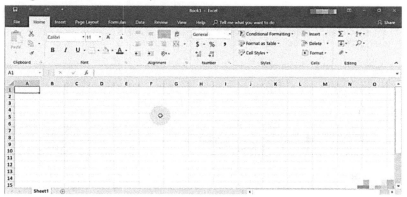

Now let's do a quick overview of the entire blank workbook screen. We will start at the top, going from left to right, then from top to bottom. First, at the upper-left corner, we have the Quick Access toolbar. It is called the Quick Access Toolbar because you can quickly access any commands on it with a single click. Whenever you hover your mouse over the Quick Access Toolbar, you will find the "Save," "shortcut," "Undo," and "Redo" icons as the default Quick Access Toolbar commands.

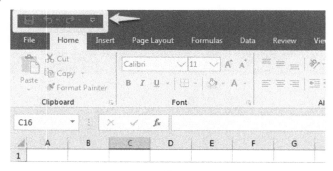

The Quick Access Toolbar can be customized to add or remove commands to and from it. We will look at steps to do that later in the book. However, when you move to the right from the Quick Access Toolbar, we have the title bar.

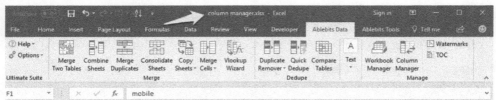

The title bar displays the name with which you save your workbook. Over to the right of the title of your worksheet is the name of the program (i.e., Excel). Moving further to the right, we have the ribbon display options, which will also cover in details later.

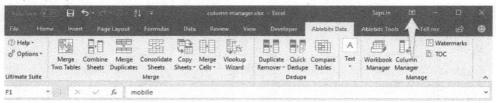

Also, to the right, we have the window options to minimize Window, restore Window or to close out of the program altogether.

Moving down, we have the Menu bar (Ribbon), which holds several tabs (File, Home, Insert, Page Layout, Formulas, Data, Review, View and Help). These tabs hold several commands which are broken into groups for easy search for command tools.

Home Tab

The Home tab holds the most used and popular commands like the cut, copy, paste, bold, italics, underline, etc. These commands within the Home tab are grouped into clipboard, font, alignment, Number, Styles, Cells and Editing. The font group is used for formatting text; for instance, the "B" means bold, "I" for italics and "U" is used for Underlining text.

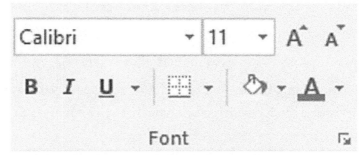

Font size and style of text are also formatted within the 'Font' group. Other actions taken under the font tool include changing background colors with the aid of the "Shading" tool and that of text using the "Font color" icon.

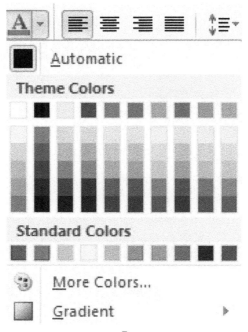

You also have the "Clipboard" for cutting, copying, and pasting your data. The 'alignment' group comes in handy when you want to align the contents of a cell(s) to either right, left, or center.

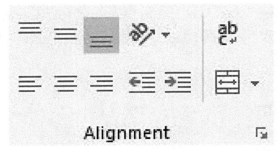

Some of these groups have an Expandable dialogue box button at the lower right-hand corner used for opening more commands that are not displayed with the group.

Insert tab

The insert tab is for inserting things like pictures, shapes, charts, sparklines, tables, etc.

Page Layout

This has to do with setting up different page orientations, themes and sheet options.

Worksheet

Below the 'Clipboard' group under the Home tab on the left-hand side, we have the 'name box.' The name box tells you the name of the cell you are currently.

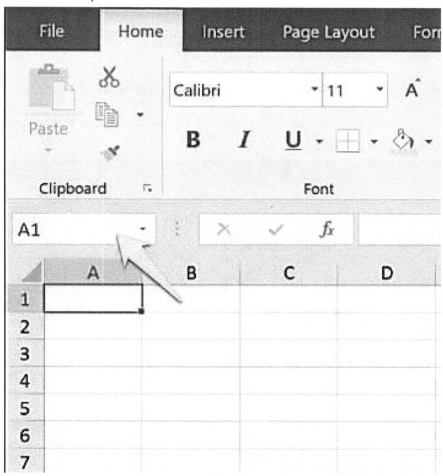

At the top of the worksheet is the column headers, which are alphabetical, beginning with A, B, C, D, E, F, etc.

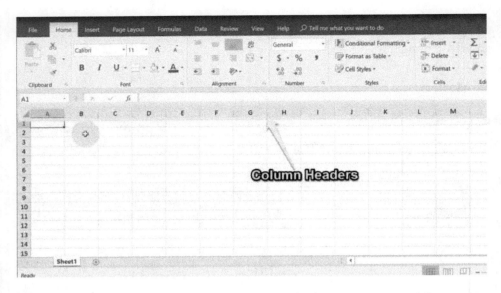

At the side, we have the Row headers, which are numerical beginning with 1,2,3,4,5,6,7, etc.

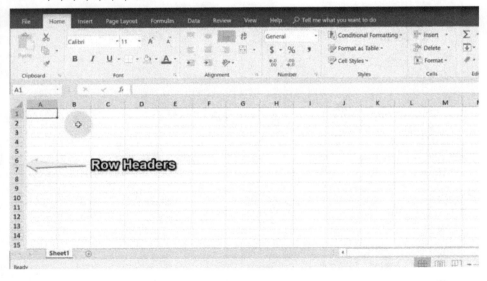

Whenever you click on any cell on the Excel worksheet, the row address and the column address of the selected cell is displayed in the name box. For instance, if you click on a cell under the H column and row 8, H8 will be displayed in the Name box, indicating that you have highlighted a cell under column H, Row 8, and the cell's name is H8.

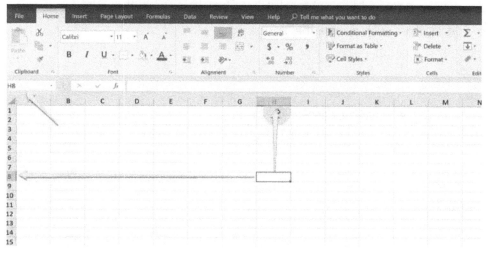

Go ahead and click any cell and look up in the name box what cell address is indicated. The name box can also be used to jump to a cell by typing the address of the cell in it. For instance, if you wish to jump the cell "B2," go ahead and type it in the name box, and the cell B2 will be highlighted on the worksheet. On the other hand, you can go to cell A1 by either typing A1 in the name box or using the short cut key "Ctrl + Home" on the keyboard. To the right of the name box, we have the formula bar.

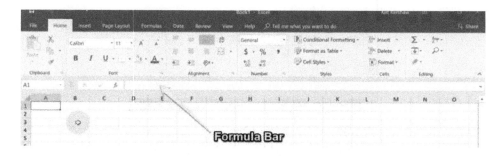

The formula bar shows you the entire content of a cell. You can also edit text or any content of a cell from the formula bar.

9

Creating Additional Worksheet

You can create additional worksheets by clicking on the "plus (+)" symbol at the bottom, just above the status bar.

Status Bar

Down below the worksheet is the Status bar. The Status bars provide information concerning the current status of the active Excel worksheet. However, whatever is displayed on the status bar can be customized. To customize the status bar, right-click on the bar and scroll down or up to see more customizable options.

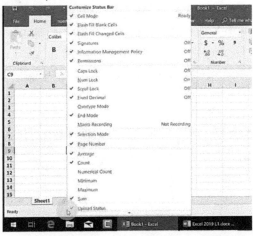

Select all the Status bar options you want to be displayed on the Status bar. For instance, if you have "SUM" selected, on the customize status bar list, it means if you select a range of cells (two or more cells) with values, it will automatically provide the calculation of the total of the content of the selected cells on the status bar. If you don't want this displayed on the status bar, uncheck it from the "customize status bar." Other functions that can be added to the status bar are minimum (the lowest values within a range of cells), maximum (the highest values within a range of cells), etc. We will cover them in detail later on when we discuss functions.

To the right of the status bar are different available views - e.g., Normal, page layout and page break preview. These options can also be found on the View tab. Over to the right, you have the Zoom feature, with 100% being the default.

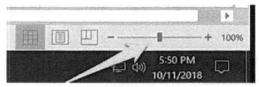

You can zoom in or zoom-out by sliding the zoom tab to the right or left, respectively. You can also customize the zoom percentage to an exact number by clicking on the Zoom tab, then click "OK" when done.

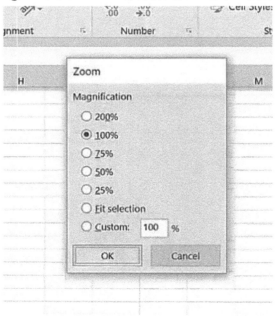

Chapter Two

Excel Basics

Customizing Excel Environment

The Microsoft Excel environment or worksheet is customizable. For example, every time a new workbook is created, you get a default font type, font size (Calibri and 11, respectively), and a single worksheet. If you wish to have a new default font style and size whenever you open a new workbook, click on File > scroll down and click on Options. This opens up the Excel Options. On the left-hand side of the 'Excel Options' window are list of customizable categories (General, Formulas, Data, Proofing, Save, Language, Ease of Access, Advanced, customize Ribbon, Quick Access Toolbar, Add-ins and Trust Center).

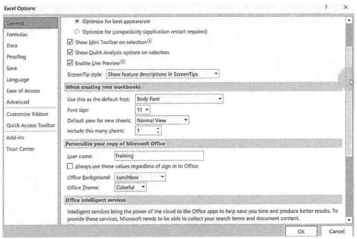

Next, Click on General > scroll to the section called 'When creating new workbooks' > Change the default font style, font size, default view for new sheets and the number of sheets that should be created whenever a new workbook is created > Click OK. You will get a prompt to close and restart Microsoft Excel so that the changes can take effect, click OK to continue. Re-open Excel again and you will realize that your new settings have taken effect.

Customizing the Quick Access Toolbar

At the top-right corner of your Excel window, you have the quick access toolbar. It is called that because you can access any command on it with a single click as opposed to accessing the command via the taskbar. You can add commands to the quick access toolbar in several ways. One of the methods is to click on the drop-down arrow to access a list of some of the more commonly used commands you can add to the quick access toolbar (e.g., New Open, Save, Undo, Redo, etc.).

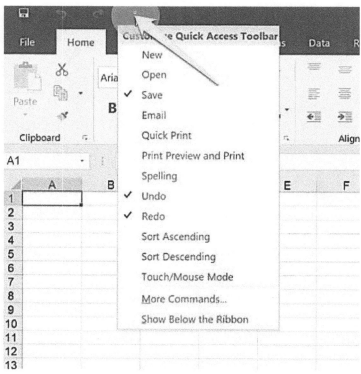

Any of the commands you select from the 'customize quick access toolbar' drop menu will be added to the Quick Access Command Toolbar. You can

13

have access to more Excel Options to add to the quick access toolbar by clicking 'More Commands' on the drop-down menu.

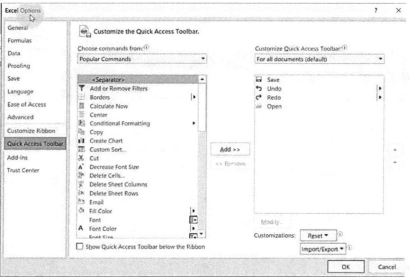

Alternatively, you can access the Excel Options by clicking Files › Options › Quick Access Toolbar. On the left of the Excel Options window, you have the Popular commands and on the right are the list of commands already added to the Quick Access Toolbar. To add any of the commands on the popular commands list to the 'quick access toolbar,' click on the command and click 'Add.'

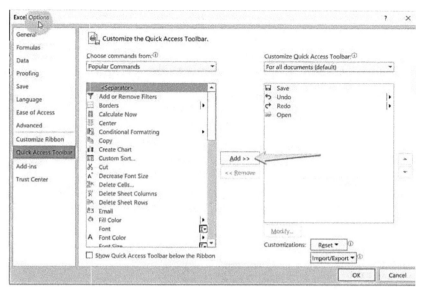

If the command you wish to add to the Quick Access Toolbar is not listed under the 'popular commands,' click the drop-down menu and select "All Commands." Scroll down to the command you wish to add, click on it and finally click on the "Add" button. Alternatively, you can double click on a command you wish to add to the Quick Access Toolbar to add it. To remove a command from the 'Quick Access Toolbar,' click on the command and click on the "Remove" button.

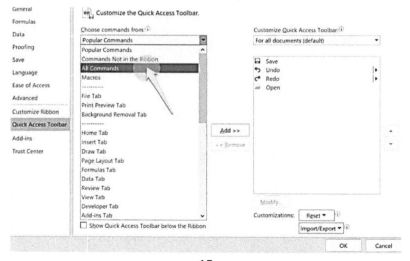

You can also swap between commands on the Quick Access Toolbar. For instance, on the previous Excel Options image, the "Save" command is the first command. You can decide to move it to the second position and make the "Undo" Command the first. To do that, click on the "Save" command and click on the Down arrow at the side.

Use this method to swap between different commands on the Quick Access Toolbar. Finally, you can use the "Separator" command to demarcate between the various commands on the Quick Access Toolbar. What you do is to add a separator in between each command.

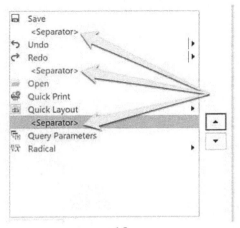

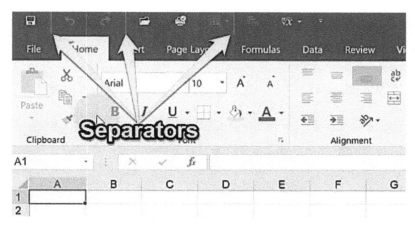

You can add as many separators as you wish to space out the commands individually or in groups. Another way to add a command to the Quick Access Toolbar is to right-click on the command on the menu bar and select "Add to Quick Access Toolbar."

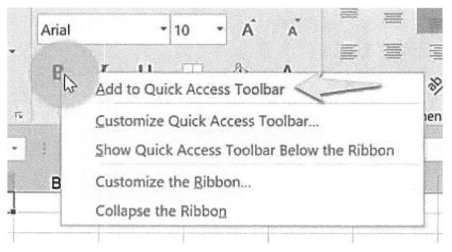

You can also add a group of commands to the 'Quick Access Toolbar.' For instance, if you wish to add the entire font command to the Quick Access Toolbar, right-click on a blank area within the font menu and click on "Add to Quick Access Toolbar." This will create an icon to represent that group of commands." To remove commands directly from the Quick Access Toolbar, right-click on the command and click "Remove from Quick Access

Toolbar." This method is also used for eliminating "Separators" from the 'Quick Access Toolbar.'

Saving A Workbook

It is a good idea to save your workbook the first few minutes after entering your data into the worksheet to prevent losing your information in case something happens. A generic name e.g., "Book1" which is displayed on the title bar, is given to your spreadsheet whenever you open a new workbook. When you save this worksheet for the first time, it comes up with a "Save As" option. The "Save As" option prompts you to select where your file should be saved and what name should replace the generic name "Book1." There are three ways to save a workbook for the first time. Firstly, if you have the "Save" button on the "Quick Access Toolbar," click on it. Alternatively, click "File" > "Save." Or you can press the F12 key on your keyboard. This will open up the "Save As" window.

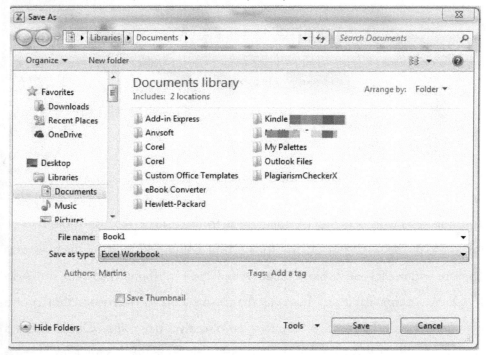

On the "Save As" window, you have the navigation pane on the left side - where you can select a location to save the workbook. On the right are subfolders within the different locations. For instance, if you wish to save it on the Desktop, click on "Desktop" on the navigation pane and click the "Save" button. If you want to save the worksheet in a folder on the Desktop, select Desktop on the left, then select the folder you wish to save it on the right. You can also choose other locations, including a flash drive (if attached) on the navigation pane to save your file. Moving down the "Save As" window is the "File name." You will realize that the default file name "Book1" is what you find there, change it to any name you wish to save your file as. Finally, click the "Save" button. When you are done, it updates the title bar to the new file name, and any time you make any changes to the worksheet and click on the "Save" button, it won't bring up the "Save As" window anymore because it now knows where to save it.

Saving A Workbook without Closing the Entire Program

To close a workbook without closing the entire Excel program, click on "File" > scroll down and click "Close." This will close your current workbook without exiting Excel. The shortcut keys to do this is "Ctrl + W."

Accessing Recent Worksheets

Accessing recent Excel files is quite easy, first, right-clicking on the Excel Program pinned to the taskbar and you would find all your recent works, click on the worksheet you wish to open. To pin the Excel Program to the taskbar, open the program > right-click on the icon of the program on the taskbar > select "pin this program to taskbar." To unpin it, right-click on the pinned program and select "unpin this program from taskbar." Alternatively, you can access your recent worksheets by clicking on "File" > "Open," and you will find all your recently used files on the right.

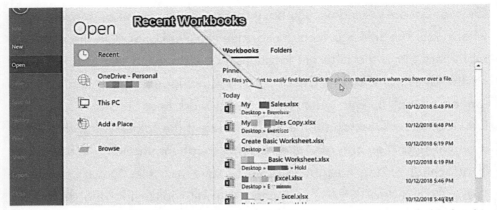

You can pin a workbook in the Recent file folder at the top of the list by hovering your mouse pointer over the worksheet title and clicking on the "pin this item to the list icon" ⊣◄ that comes up to the right.

Paste Options

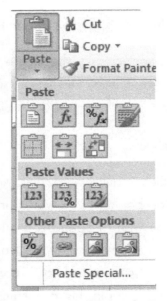

There are several paste options in Microsoft Excel – the simplistic paste option which pastes a copied function into the new cell, the values paste option which pastes the result of the copied function. Other paste options include pasting the copied item 'as picture' (this option pastes the content of a cell without changing it), linked picture (any changes made in the original cell will be updated), etc. We will look at the paste options in detail in subsequent chapters.

Inserting a Function

You can insert functions by clicking on 'Formulas' tab > insert function > then search for the function you wish to use. Click on the drop-down arrow by the "Select a category" menu to display the various categories of functions.

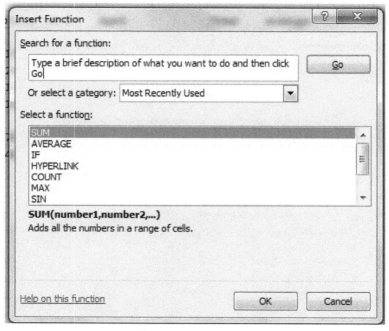

For instance, you can select the "Date & Time" function to carry out Date & Time-related activities on Excel 2019. Selecting "All" displays the entire functions available on Excel. Scroll down and select the ideal function for the calculation you intend to carry out. Under the 'Formulas' tab, functions are grouped into categories such as financial, logical, Math &

Trigonometry, Date & Time, AutoSum, as well as recently used functions in the Formulas Library.

Calculation options

Make sure workbook calculation under the 'Calculation options' is set to 'Automatic.' What this does is that previous outcome from calculations are automatically updated whenever a value used in the formula is changed or updated.

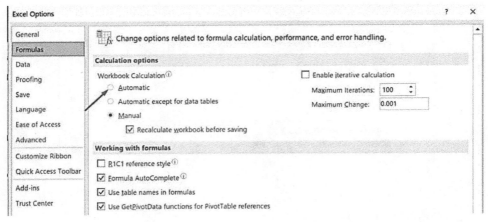

Chapter Three
Functions

When it comes to calculations in Microsoft Excel, there five key things that are relevant. They include:

- Excel's inbuilt function (formulas)
- Function Syntax
- Numbers
- Boolean statements (True or False) and
- Cell References (Cell Address)

For you to understand how to apply a formula in Excel, you must understand its syntax. Every function in Excel has a syntax and they play a pivotal role in using such function. To have a glimpse of the syntax of any function, as soon as you type the equal to sign followed by the function name and open a bracket, Excel gives you a list of arguments. For instance, let's use the SUMIF function for illustration. When you type =SUMIF(excel automatically brings up the syntax for using the formula with a list of arguments such as range, criteria and [sum_range].

Another vital thing to note when using Excel functions or formula is whenever we use criteria that are not a number, Boolean (true or false), or a cell reference; we must put them in double quotes "xxxx".

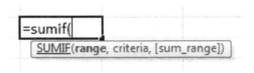

These are the inputs required by excel when using these functions to get an output. Note that contents within an angular bracket[ ] are optional. So there are instances where we will only need the range and criteria to get our calculations done. In such a case, the syntax will be =SUMIF(range, criteria).

SUM & AVERAGE Function

The SUM function is a math and trig function used for adding values. You can add individual values, cell references or ranges or a mix of all three. We can use the SUM function in our example below to add up the total sales for each employee from January to April an insert the result in Cell H8.

	F14	▾	⨍ₓ	=F13/4					
	A	B	C	D	E	F	G	H	I
1	Sales Spread sheet								
2	5/15/2020								
3									
4						Commission:		8%	
5									
6		Employee ID	January	February	March	April		Total	Average
7									
8		2437661	10110.3	11175.7	34141	15135.2			
9		2437662	22200.8	12210.6	21240.8	17205.8			
10		2347663	19210.3	15185.1	25195.1	12310.4			
11		2437664	35220.2	11195.4	30185.7	19250.1			
12									
13		Month Total	86741.5	49766.8	110763	63901.5			
14		Month Average	21685.4	12441.7	27690.6	15975.4			
15									
16									

H ◂ ▸ H Sheet1 / Sheet2 / Sheet3 / ⸦⸧

To add up the range for the employee with ID 2437661, type in the equal sign and the alphabet 'S'. This will bring up a list of functions, scroll down and select 'SUM' function or type in "SU" to go straight to functions starting with 'SU' and double click on the SUM function from the list

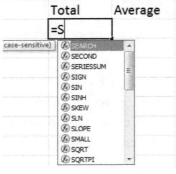

24

Double-click on the 'SUM' function when it pops up to bring SUM function syntax SUM(number 1, [number 2],.....). as shown below;

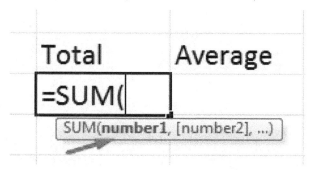

The first argument in the SUM function is a range of cells. It could be any range of cells you select from your worksheet. If you want to select additional cell ranges that are not adjacent, you type them individually. To add the range for the first employee in the SUM function, we say =SUM(first cell:last cell). This means, sum up the content of a range of cells beginning with the first cell to the last cell. The colon in this function indicates 'through.' Therefore, the formula to sum up the total sales for the first employee with identification number 2437661 is given as =SUM(C8:F8).

	A	B	C	D	E	F	G	H	I
	SUM		× ✓ fx	=SUM(C8:F8)					
1	Sales Spread sheet								
2	5/15/2020								
3									
4						Commission:		8%	
5									
6		Employee ID	January	February	March	April		Total	Average
7									
8		2437661	10110.25	11175.65	34140.96	15135.15		=SUM(C8:F8)	
9		2437662	22200.75	12210.63	21240.82	17205.79			
10		2347663	19210.34	15185.11	25195.14	12310.44			
11		2437664	35220.15	11195.37	30185.66	19250.14			
12									
13		Month Total	86741.49	49766.76	110762.6	63901.52			
14		Month Average	21685.37	12441.69	27690.65	15975.38			

Hit the Enter key on the keyboard to get the answer.

	H9			fx					
	A	B	C	D	E	F	G	H	I
1	Sales Spread sheet								
2	5/15/2020								
3									
4						Commission:		8%	
5									
6		Employee ID	January	February	March	April		Total	Average
7									
8		2437661	10110.25	11175.65	34140.96	15135.15		70562.01	
9		2437662	22200.75	12210.63	21240.82	17205.79			
10		2347663	19210.34	15185.11	25195.14	12310.44			
11		2437664	35220.15	11195.37	30185.66	19250.14			
12									
13		Month Total	86741.49	49766.76	110762.6	63901.52			
14		Month Average	21685.37	12441.69	27690.65	15975.38			
15									

You can do the same for the remaining employees. Employee 2 is calculated, thus =SUM(C9:F9), Employee 3 is calculated thus =SUM (C10 :F10), Employee 4 is calculated thus =SUM(C11:F11). Alternatively, you can copy the content of the result of the first calculation and paste in subsequent cells for Employee 2 to Employee 4.

	E18			fx					
	A	B	C	D	E	F	G	H	I
1	Sales Spread sheet								
2	5/15/2020								
3									
4						Commission:		8%	
5									
6		Employee ID	January	February	March	April		Total	Average
7									
8		2437661	10110.25	11175.65	34140.96	15135.15		70562.01	
9		2437662	22200.75	12210.63	21240.82	17205.79		72857.99	
10		2347663	19210.34	15185.11	25195.14	12310.44		71901.03	
11		2437664	35220.15	11195.37	30185.66	19250.14		95851.32	
12									
13		Month Total	86741.49	49766.76	110762.6	63901.52			
14		Month Average	21685.37	12441.69	27690.65	15975.38			

Copying and pasting the values from the first calculation into subsequent cells to get their total may be okay if the data you are working on is not much. It becomes time-consuming when you are working on data with an extensive range of values. In such a case, hover your cursor around the auto fill handle at the lower-right corner of the first cell in the range until a black plus sign appears.

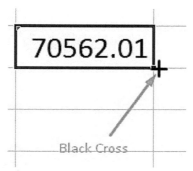

Black Cross

With the plus sign turned black, drag the autofill handle (black square box at the lower-right corner) down to cover all the cells you want the formula used for the first calculation to be applied to. Alternatively, double-click on the autofill handle.

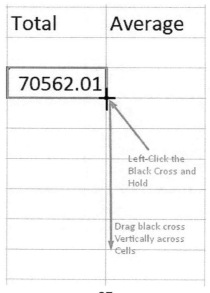

This will paste the result in each cell based on the formula used in calculating the content of the first cell. We can also perform what is called a Range-to-Range function. In this case, instead of referencing the address of the cells in the formula, we can use the range-to-range option. For instance, instead of writing the formula to calculate the total sales for January as =SUM(C8:C11), we can write it thus =SUM(C:C) without referring to the row address. What this does is to make the formula dynamic. If there are any changes in figures within the January sales, the result is automatically updated. This way, you don't need to key in the formula whenever there is an adjustment of a figure(s).

Total	Average
70562.01	
72857.99	
71901.03	
95851.32	

AVERAGE Function

The Average function returns the average (arithmetic mean) of the arguments, which can be numbers, arrays, or references that contain values. The general syntax for the Average function is given thus;

=AVERAGE(argument1,argument2,argument3,…) or

=AVERAGE(range1,range2,range3,…)

We can now calculate the Average for each employee from January – April.

=AVERAGEC8:F8)										
	A	B	C	D	E	F	G	H	I	J	K
1	Sales Spread sheet										
2	5/15/2020										
3											
4						Commission:		8%			
5											
6		Employee ID	January	February	March	April		Total	Average		
7											
8		2437661	10110.25	11175.65	34140.96	15135.15		70562.01	=AVERAGEC8:F8)		
9		2437662	22200.75	12210.63	21240.82	17205.79		72857.99			
10		2347663	19210.34	15185.11	25195.14	12310.44		71901.03			
11		2437664	35220.15	11195.37	30185.66	19250.14		95851.32			
12											
13		Month Total	86741.49	49766.76	110762.6	63901.52					
14		Month Average	21685.37	12441.69	27690.65	15975.38					

When you hit the ENTER key on the keyboard, you get the average sales from January – April for Employee with ID 2347661.

	A	B	C	D	E	F	G	H	I	J	K
1	Sales Spread sheet										
2	5/15/2020										
3											
4						Commission:		8%			
5											
6		Employee ID	January	February	March	April		Total	Average		
7											
8		2437661	10110.25	11175.65	34140.96	15135.15		70562.01	17640.5		
9		2437662	22200.75	12210.63	21240.82	17205.79		72857.99			
10		2347663	19210.34	15185.11	25195.14	12310.44		71901.03			
11		2437664	35220.15	11195.37	30185.66	19250.14		95851.32			
12											
13		Month Total	86741.49	49766.76	110762.6	63901.52					
14		Month Average	21685.37	12441.69	27690.65	15975.38					

Next, copy the figures in Cell I8 and paste in I9, I10 and I11 or double-click on the autofill handle with a black plus sign to obtain the Average sales for the remaining employees.

	A	B	C	D	E	F	G	H	I	J	K	L	M
1	Sales Spread sheet												
2	5/15/2020												
3													
4						Commission:		8%					
5													
6		Employee ID	January	February	March	April		Total	Average				
7													
8		2437661	10110.25	11175.65	34140.96	15135.15		70562.01	17640.5				
9		2437662	22200.75	12210.63	21240.82	17205.79		72857.99	18214.5				
10		2347663	19210.34	15185.11	25195.14	12310.44		71901.03	17975.26		Average Sales for		
11		2437664	35220.15	11195.37	30185.66	19250.14		95851.32	23962.83		all the Employees		
12													
13		Month Total	86741.49	49766.76	110762.6	63901.52							
14		Month Average	21685.37	12441.69	27690.65	15975.38							
15													

RANK.AVG Function

The **RANK.AVG** Function returns the rank of a number in a list of numbers with a size relative to other values in the list; if more than one value has the same rank, the average rank is returned. The general syntax is

$$=RANK.AVG(number,ref,[order])$$

For illustration, let's use the RANK.AVG function for the gross salaries in our Midas Concept LLC Payroll example.

	A	B	C	D	E	F	G	H	I	J
1						Midas Concept LLC				
2						Payroll				
3	Employee No	First Name	Last Name	SSN	Department	Employment Date	Hour	Rate	Gross	RANK.AVG
4	b2437110	Mark	Spencer	450012432	Admin	1/22/2019	50	$75.00	$3,000.00	
5	b2437111	John	Bolt	341112434	Sales	7/24/2019	50	$44.30	$1,772.00	
6	a2437112	James	Phrase	670022435	Sales	2/24/2018	52	$19.90	$835.00	
7	b2437113	Luther	Miles	882012539	Marketing	6/3/2017	58	$15.00	$1,770.00	
8	2437114	Harry	Cliton	553112632	Sales	12/28/2019	58	$55.50	$1,623.00	
9	2437115	Bells	Simpson	125512442	Personnel	1/5/2017	45	$12.00	$430.00	
10	b2437116	Bob	Kelly	522001248	Human Resource	8/23/2019	45	$12.00	$430.00	
11	b2437117	Martins	April	538012498	Sales	8/13/2018	58	$15.50	$1,807.00	
12	2437118	James	Kingsley	587012489	Admin	9/27/2018	58	$49.00	$1,960.00	
13	2437119	Robert	Hume	480026440	Sales	10/7/2019	30	$55.95	$1,808.00	
14	b2437120	Harold	Jason	552812450	Sales	8/30/2019	30	$45.20	$1,920	
15	b2437121	David	Kessington	421596508	Sales	2/11/2019	25	$33.16	$1,025.85	
16	b2437122	Davis	Gray	207843531	Marketing	3/27/2017	30	$32.64	$1,012.66	
17	a2437123	Benjamin	Samuel	317960683	Marketing	5/7/2018	25	$32.12	$999.47	
18	a2437124	Anderson	Smith	527728054	Sales	2/21/2018	45	$31.59	$986.28	
19	a2437125	Wright	Clark	200968363	Director	7/17/2017	29	$31.07	$973.09	
20	a2437126	Mitchell	Johnson	523191905	Procurement	5/14/2017	32	$30.54	$959.90	
21	a2437127	Thomas	Rodriguez	213597710	Sales	11/24/2016	45	$30.02	$946.71	
22	a2437128	Jackson	Perez	519214366	Marketing	12/9/2017	56	$29.50	$1,867.00	

Note: We will be using the Midas Concept LLC Payroll for most of our illustrations in this book, complete data for this payroll is attached as Appendix 2.

Use the formula

$$=RANK.AVG(I4,I:I)$$

The above gives us **RANK.AVG** Gross of 2 for the first employee when we hit the ENTER key.

We can now check for the other employees by hovering and double-clicking on the autofill handle.

AVERAGEA Function

The **AVERAGEA function** returns the average of cells containing numbers as well as text or characters or both. To calculate the average of a cell range that does not hold numbers, Excel adds the numeric value or each value together and divides the total number of values specified. That is average true as one (1) and false as Zero (0). What this means is that if there is any data available in a cell, it will calculate that as one (1). However, if there is no data available in a cell, it will calculate that as zero, which is not added up or divide. A perfect example is our Midas Concept LLC payroll, where we have the Employee number. Note that some employee numbers have an alphabet as their prefix, while others don't.

Employee No	First Name	Last Name	Social Security Number	Date of Employment	Hour	Rate	Gross
				Midas Concept LLC			
				Payroll			
b2437110	Mark	Spencer	450012432	1/22/2019	50	$75.00	$3,000.00
b2437111	John	Bolt	341112434	7/24/2019	50	$44.30	$1,772.00
a2437112	James	Phrase	670022435	2/24/2018	52	$19.90	$835.00
b2437113	Luther	Miles	882012539	6/3/2017		$15.00	$0.00
2437114	Harry	Cliton	553112632	12/28/2019		$55.50	$0.00
2437115	Bells	Simpson	125512442	1/5/2017	45	$12.00	$430.00
b2437116	Bob	Kelly	522001248	8/23/2019	45	$12.00	$430.00
b2437117	Martins	April	538012498	8/13/2018		$15.50	$0.00
2437118	James	Kingsley	587012489	9/27/2018	30	$49.00	$1,960.00
2437119	Robert	Hume	480026440	10/7/2019	30	$55.95	$1,808.00
b2437120	Harold	Jason	552812450	8/30/2019	30	$45.20	$1,920
b2437121	David	Kessington	421596508	2/11/2019	25	$33.16	$1,025.85
b2437122	Davis	Gray	207843531	3/27/2017	30	$32.64	$1,012.66

It is easy to perform an AVERAGEA function on the gross salaries column because there is no empty cell on that column. However, if we perform an AVERAGEA function on the Employee No column, it will add up all the cells (including those with numbers only and those having text and numbers together) and divides it by the total number of cells. But if there are empty cells within the employee no' or 'Hour' column, it marks any empty cell as false and does not use them for any of the calculations.

So we say

$$=\text{AVERAGEA}(A:A)$$

Or

$$=\text{AVERAGEA}(F:F)$$

This gives use the average value of the cell range with content.

AVERAGEIF Function

AVERAGEIF function returns the average of selected arguments specified by some given criteria. This function finds the average of data if the given conditions are fulfilled. In our example, we will be looking for the average salaries paid to the employees who worked for 30 hours. The General syntax for AVERAGEIF Function is given thus;

$$\text{AVERAGEIF}(\text{range,criteria[average\_range]})$$

Where range is the column where our criteria sits,
Criteria is the condition to be fulfilled, Average_range is the target column. So for our calculation, we say;

$$=\text{AVERAGEIF}(F:F,50,H:H)$$

From our example, F:F is the column where our condition sits; our condition is to calculate the average salaries for all employee who has worked for 50 hours. So 50 is the condition. And H:H is the target column where the action will take place. The action is to calculate the average of the Gross of employees with 50 hours.

Midas Concept LLC
Payroll

Last Name	Social Security Number	Date of Employment	Hour	Rate	Gross		AVERAGEIF
Spencer	450012432	1/22/2019	50	$75.00	$3,000.00		=AVERAGEIF(F:F,50,H:H)
Bolt	341112434	7/24/2019	50	$44.30	$1,772.00		
Phrase	670022435	2/24/2018	52	$19.90	$835.00		
Miles	882012539	6/3/2017		$15.00	$0.00		
Cliton	553112632	12/28/2019		$55.50	$0.00		2
Simpson	125512442	1/5/2017	45	$12.00	$430.00		
Kelly	522001248	8/23/2019	45	$12.00	$430.00		
April	538012498	8/13/2018		$15.50	$0.00		
Kingsley	587012489	9/27/2018	30	$49.00	$1,960.00		
Hume	480026440	10/7/2019	30	$55.95	$1,808.00		
Jason	552812450	8/30/2019	30	$45.20	$1,920		

We have an answer of $2386

Midas Concept LLC
Payroll

Last Name	Social Security Number	Date of Employment	Hour	Rate	Gross		AVERAGEIF
Spencer	450012432	1/22/2019	50	$75.00	$3,000.00		2386
Bolt	341112434	7/24/2019	50	$44.30	$1,772.00		
Phrase	670022435	2/24/2018	52	$19.90	$835.00		
Miles	882012539	6/3/2017		$15.00	$0.00		
Cliton	553112632	12/28/2019		$55.50	$0.00		
Simpson	125512442	1/5/2017	45	$12.00	$430.00		
Kelly	522001248	8/23/2019	45	$12.00	$430.00		
April	538012498	8/13/2018		$15.50	$0.00		
Kingsley	587012489	9/27/2018	30	$49.00	$1,960.00		
Hume	480026440	10/7/2019	30	$55.95	$1,808.00		
Jason	552812450	8/30/2019	30	$45.20	$1,920		

SUMIF Function

The SUMIF function sums a range of cells based on a single condition or criteria. The syntax for the SUMIF function is given as

$$=SUMIF(range,criteria,[sum\_range])$$

Where range is the range of cells, you want to be evaluated. Criteria is the criteria in the form of a number, expression, or text that defines which cells will be added. For example, criteria can be expressed as 40, "40", ">40", "<40", "oranges" etc. while the Sum range is the actual cells to sum. Let's use our Midas Concept Payroll for this illustration. We want to find out the Gross Salary paid to employees that worked for 30 hours.

Employee	First Name	Last Name	Social Security Number	Date of Employment	Hour	Rate	Gross
			Midas Concept LLC				
			Payroll				
2437110	Mark	Spencer	SS 450012432	1/22/2019	50	$75.00	$3,000.00
2437111	John	Bolt	341112434	7/24/2019	50	$44.30	$1,772.00
2437112	James	Phrase	670022435	2/24/2018	52	$19.90	$835.00
2437113	Luther	Miles	882012539	6/3/2017		$15.00	$0.00
2437114	Harry	Cliton	553112632	12/28/2019		$55.50	$0.00
2437115	Bells	Simpson	125512442	1/5/2017	45	$12.00	$430.00
2437116	Bob	Kelly	522001248	8/23/2019	45	$12.00	$430.00
2437117	Martins	April	538012498	8/13/2018		$15.50	$0.00
2437118	James	Kingsley	587012489	9/27/2018	30	$49.00	$1,960.00
2437119	Robert	Hume	480026440	10/7/2019	30	$55.95	$1,808.00
2437120	Harold	Jason	552812450	8/30/2019	30	$45.20	$1,920
2437121	David	Kessington	421596508	2/11/2019	25	$33.16	$1,025.85
2437122	Davis	Gray	207843531	3/27/2017	30	$32.64	$1,012.66
2437123	Benjamin	Samuel	317960683	5/7/2018	25	$32.12	$999.47
2437124	Anderson	Smith	527728054	2/21/2018	45	$31.59	$986.28

Midas Concept Payroll Sales Commission for Midas Contacts Book Sales for the Year

We Say;

$$=SUMIF(F29:F43,30,H29:H43)$$

Recall that the syntax for SUM is given as =SUMIF(range,criteria,[sum_range])

Where F29:F43 from our Midas Concept payroll is the cell range we are working with. 30 is the criteria. That is we are looking for the total salaries of those that worked for 30 hours and H29:H43 is the sum_range. Which means the sum the Gross for employees with 30 hours only.

SUM   ✗ ✓ ƒx =SUMIF(F29:F43,30,H29:H43)

First Name	Last Name	Social Security Number	Date of Employment	Hour	Rate	Gross			
		Midas Concept LLC							
		Payroll							
Mark	Spencer	SS 450012432	1/22/2019	50	$75.00	$3,000.00		=SUMIF(F29:F43,30,H29:H43)	
John	Bolt	341112434	7/24/2019	50	$44.30	$1,772.00			
James	Phrase	670022435	2/24/2018	52	$19.90	$835.00			
Luther	Miles	882012539	6/3/2017		$15.00	$0.00			
Harry	Cliton	553112632	12/28/2019		$55.50	$0.00			
Bells	Simpson	125512442	1/5/2017	45	$12.00	$430.00			
Bob	Kelly	522001248	8/23/2019	45	$12.00	$430.00			
Martins	April	538012498	8/13/2018		$15.50	$0.00			
James	Kingsley	587012489	9/27/2018	30	$49.00	$1,960.00			
Robert	Hume	480026440	10/7/2019	30	$55.95	$1,808.00			
Harold	Jason	552812450	8/30/2019	30	$45.20	$1,920			
David	Kessington	421596508	2/11/2019	25	$33.16	$1,025.85			
Davis	Gray	207843531	3/27/2017	30	$32.64	$1,012.66			
Benjamin	Samuel	317960683	5/7/2018	25	$32.12	$999.47			
Anderson	Smith	527728054	2/21/2018	45	$31.59	$986.28			

The total amount for employees that worked for 30 hours is $6700.664.

	B	C	D	E	F	G	H	I	J
26				**Midas Concept LLC**					
27				Payroll					
28	First Name	Last Name	Social Security Number	Date of Employment	Hour	Rate	Gross		
29	Mark	Spencer	SS 450012432	1/22/2019	50	$75.00	$3,000.00		6700.664
30	John	Bolt	341112434	7/24/2019	50	$44.30	$1,772.00		
31	James	Phrase	670022435	2/24/2018	52	$19.90	$835.00		
32	Luther	Miles	882012539	6/3/2017		$15.00	$0.00		
33	Harry	Cliton	553112632	12/28/2019		$55.50	$0.00		
34	Bells	Simpson	125512442	1/5/2017	45	$12.00	$430.00		
35	Bob	Kelly	522001248	8/23/2019	45	$12.00	$430.00		
36	Martins	April	538012498	8/13/2018		$15.50	$0.00		
37	James	Kingsley	587012489	9/27/2019	30	$49.00	$1,960.00		
38	Robert	Hume	480026440	10/7/2019	30	$55.95	$1,808.00		
39	Harold	Jason	552812450	8/30/2019	30	$45.20	$1,920		
40	David	Kessington	421596508	2/11/2019	25	$33.16	$1,025.85		
41	Davis	Gray	207843531	3/27/2017	30	$32.64	$1,012.66		
42	Benjamin	Samuel	317960683	5/7/2018	25	$32.12	$999.47		
43	Anderson	Smith	527728054	2/21/2018	45	$31.59	$986.28		

For our second illustration with the SUMIF function, we will find the Gross for all employees earning $12 per hour from our Midas Concept payroll. To do this we recall the syntax for SUMIF function is

=SUMIF(range,criteria,[sum_range]).

The formula for this

=SUMIF(G29:G43,12,H29:H43)

Where;

The range is G29:G43, the Criteria is 12. Note that we didn't add the dollar symbol because Excel sees the content of the column as numbers and not a combinations of numbers and special character. The Sum_range is H29:H43

	B	C	D	E	F	G	H	I	J	K	L
	SUM	▾ × ✓ fx	=SUMIF(G29:G43,12,H29:H43)								
26				**Midas Concept LLC**							
27				Payroll							
28	First Name	Last Name	Social Security Number	Date of Employment	Hour	Rate	Gross				
29	Mark	Spencer	450012432	1/22/2019	50	$75.00	$3,000.00		6700.664		
30	John	Bolt	341112434	7/24/2019	50	$44.30	$1,772.00				
31	James	Phrase	670022435	2/24/2018	52	$19.90	$835.00		=SUMIF(G29:G43,12,H29:H43)		
32	Luther	Miles	882012539	6/3/2017		$15.00	$0.00		SUMIF(range, criteria, [sum_range])		
33	Harry	Cliton	553112632	12/28/2019		$55.50	$0.00				
34	Bells	Simpson	125512442	1/5/2017	45	$12.00	$430.00				
35	Bob	Kelly	522001248	8/23/2019	45	$12.00	$430.00				
36	Martins	April	538012498	8/13/2018		$15.50	$0.00				
37	James	Kingsley	587012489	9/27/2019	30	$49.00	$1,960.00				
38	Robert	Hume	480026440	10/7/2019	30	$55.95	$1,808.00				
39	Harold	Jason	552812450	8/30/2019	30	$45.20	$1,920				
40	David	Kessington	421596508	2/11/2019	25	$33.16	$1,025.85				
41	Davis	Gray	207843531	3/27/2017	30	$32.64	$1,012.66				
42	Benjamin	Samuel	317960683	5/7/2018	25	$32.12	$999.47				
43	Anderson	Smith	527728054	2/21/2018	45	$31.59	$986.28				

The total Gross Salary for employees earning $12 per hour is $860.

First Name	Last Name	Social Security Number	Date of Employment	Hour	Rate	Gross		
			Midas Concept LLC					
			Payroll					
Mark	Spencer	450012432	1/22/2019	50	$75.00	$3,000.00		6701
John	Bolt	341112434	7/24/2019	50	$44.30	$1,772.00		
James	Phrase	670022435	2/24/2018	52	$19.90	$835.00		860
Luther	Miles	882012539	6/3/2017		$15.00	$0.00		
Harry	Cliton	553112632	12/28/2019		$55.50	$0.00		
Bells	Simpson	125512442	1/5/2017	45	$12.00	$430.00		
Bob	Kelly	522001248	8/23/2019	45	$12.00	$430.00		
Martins	April	538012498	8/13/2018		$15.50	$0.00		
James	Kingsley	587012489	9/27/2018	30	$49.00	$1,960.00		
Robert	Hume	480026440	10/7/2019	30	$55.95	$1,808.00		
Harold	Jason	552812450	8/30/2019	30	$45.20	$1,920		
David	Kessington	421596508	2/11/2019	25	$33.16	$1,025.85		
Davis	Gray	207843531	3/27/2017	30	$32.64	$1,012.66		
Benjamin	Samuel	317960683	5/7/2018	25	$32.12	$999.47		
Anderson	Smith	527728054	2/21/2018	45	$31.59	$986.28		

Let's look at another SUMIF example. This time around, we look for the total salary paid to employees whose salary is more than $1000. In this example, the [Sum_Range] is not required to obtain the result. Since the addition of sum_range is optional for this illustration, Excel will automatically consider the 'criteria' and the 'range' only. So in our example, our criteria will be greater than $1000 (>$1000).

=SUMIF(H29:H43,">$1000")

Recall that when using Excel functions or formula and the criteria is not a number, Boolean (true or false), or cell reference, they are placed within double quotes "xxxx". So > $1000 is not any of the mentioned, hence is placed in double-quotes.

SUM		fx =SUMIF(H29:H43,">$1000")									
First Name	Last Name	Social Security Number	Date of Employment	Hour	Rate	Gross					
			Midas Concept LLC								
			Payroll								
Mark	Spencer	450012432	1/22/2019	50	$75.00	$3,000.00		6701			
John	Bolt	341112434	7/24/2019	50	$44.30	$1,772.00					
James	Phrase	670022435	2/24/2018	52	$19.90	$835.00		860			
Luther	Miles	882012539	6/3/2017		$15.00	$0.00					
Harry	Cliton	553112632	12/28/2019		$55.50	$0.00	=SUMIF(H29:H43,">$1000")				
Bells	Simpson	125512442	1/5/2017	45	$12.00	$430.00	SUMIF(range, criteria, [sum_range])				
Bob	Kelly	522001248	8/23/2019	45	$12.00	$430.00					
Martins	April	538012498	8/13/2018		$15.50	$0.00					
James	Kingsley	587012489	9/27/2018	30	$49.00	$1,960.00					
Robert	Hume	480026440	10/7/2019	30	$55.95	$1,808.00					
Harold	Jason	552812450	8/30/2019	30	$45.20	$1,920					
David	Kessington	421596508	2/11/2019	25	$33.16	$1,025.85					
Davis	Gray	207843531	3/27/2017	30	$32.64	$1,012.66					
Benjamin	Samuel	317960683	5/7/2018	25	$32.12	$999.47					
Anderson	Smith	527728054	2/21/2018	45	$31.59	$986.28					

The answer for the total employees earning salaries above $1000 is $12499.

First Name	Last Name	Social Security Number	Date of Employment	Hour	Rate	Gross		
			Midas Concept LLC					
			Payroll					
Mark	Spencer	450012432	1/22/2019	50	$75.00	$3,000.00	6701	
John	Bolt	341112434	7/24/2019	50	$44.30	$1,772.00		
James	Phrase	670022435	2/24/2018	52	$19.90	$835.00	860	
Luther	Miles	882012539	6/3/2017		$15.00	$0.00		
Harry	Cliton	553112632	12/28/2019		$55.50	$0.00	12499	
Beils	Simpson	125512442	1/5/2017	45	$12.00	$430.00		
Bob	Kelly	522001248	8/23/2019	45	$12.00	$430.00		
Martins	April	538012498	8/13/2018		$15.50	$0.00		
James	Kingsley	587012489	9/27/2018	30	$49.00	$1,960.00		
Robert	Hume	480026440	10/7/2019	30	$55.95	$1,808.00		
Harold	Jason	552812450	8/30/2019	30	$45.20	$1,920		
David	Kessington	421596508	2/11/2019	25	$33.16	$1,025.85		
Davis	Gray	207843531	3/27/2017	30	$32.64	$1,012.66		
Benjamin	Samuel	317960683	5/7/2018	25	$32.12	$999.47		
Anderson	Smith	527728054	2/21/2018	45	$31.59	$986.28		

SUMIFS Function

The SUMIFS function sums a range of cells based on more than one condition or criteria. The syntax for the SUMIFS function is given as

SUMIFS(sum_range,criteria_range1,criteria1,[criteria_range2,...)

The SUMIFS function is used to address conditions with multiple criteria. For instance, we can find the total salaries for those who earn more than $1000 and work for more than 50 hours in the Midas Concepts LLC Payroll. To start with, we have two criteria.

1. Employees who worked for more than 50 hours

2. Employees earning over $1000

The input required for the SUMIFS function are

1. Sum_range, which in our case is 'Gross Salaries.' This column has the total salaries that satisfied the given criteria

2. Criteria_range1, which in our case is 'Hour.' This column where hour criteria sit

3. Criteria1 is >50. This is the first condition that must be satisfied.

4. Criteria_range2 is 'Gross.' This is where our criteria2 sits.
5. Criteria2 in our illustration is >$1000. This is the second condition that must be satisfied.

So we have;

$$=SUMIFS(H29:H43,F29:F43,">50",H29:H43,">1000")$$

The total salary paid to employees that earn more than $1000 and have worked for more than 50 hours is $2751.76.

COUNT Function

The COUNT Function, as the name implies, counts up all the cells containing numeric data (numbers). We will be using the Payroll for Midas Concept LLC for our illustrations on how the COUNT and COUNTA functions work. For instance, on the Midas Concept payroll spreadsheet, we can identify the number of people that worked using the COUNT function.

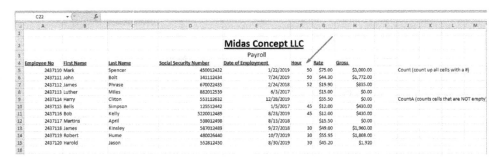

Note that we could count the number of cells under the Hour column holding numbers for the Midas Concept LLC at a glance because this is quite a small data. This won't be easy for a large organization with thousands of employees; hence the COUNT function becomes handy. To do this for the Hour column in our payroll, type in =COUNT(First cell in the range:Last cell in the range). That is, =COUNT(F5:F15), as shown below:

	D	E	F	G	H	I	J	K	L	M
1										
2		**Midas Concept LLC**								
3		Payroll								
4	Social Security Number	Date of Employment	Hour	Rate	Gross					
5	450012432	1/22/2019	50	$75.00	$3,000.00		Count (count up all cells with a #)			
6	341112434	7/24/2019	50	$44.30	$1,772.00		=COUNT(F5:F15)			
7	670022435	2/24/2018	52	$19.90	$835.00					
8	882012539	6/3/2017		$15.00	$0.00					
9	553112632	12/28/2019		$55.50	$0.00		CountA (counts cells that are NOT empty)			
10	125512442	1/5/2017	45	$12.00	$430.00					
11	5220012489	8/23/2019	45	$12.00	$430.00					
12	538012498	8/13/2018		$15.50	$0.00					
13	587012489	9/27/2018	30	$49.00	$1,960.00					
14	480026440	10/7/2019	30	$55.95	$1,808.00					
15	552812450	8/30/2019	30	$45.20	$1,920					
16										

For our illustration, the cell which has numbers under the hour column is 8. Three cells within that column are empty.

H17   *fx*

	D	E	F	G	H	I	J	K	L	M
1										
2		**Midas Concept LLC**								
3		Payroll								
4	Social Security Number	Date of Employment	Hour	Rate	Gross					
5	450012432	1/22/2019	50	$75.00	$3,000.00		Count (count up all cells with a #)			
6	341112434	7/24/2019	50	$44.30	$1,772.00		8			
7	670022435	2/24/2018	52	$19.90	$835.00					
8	882012539	6/3/2017		$15.00	$0.00					
9	553112632	12/28/2019		$55.50	$0.00		CountA (counts cells that are NOT empty			
10	125512442	1/5/2017	45	$12.00	$430.00					
11	5220012489	8/23/2019	45	$12.00	$430.00					
12	538012498	8/13/2018		$15.50	$0.00					
13	587012489	9/27/2018	30	$49.00	$1,960.00					
14	480026440	10/7/2019	30	$55.95	$1,808.00					
15	552812450	8/30/2019	30	$45.20	$1,920					
16										

Note that the COUNT function only deals with numbers and not alphabets. It would not count cells containing alphabets. Also, don't confuse the COUNT function with the count on the Status bar, the Count on the Status bar deals with the number of cells that contain data (i.e., alphabets and numbers) while the count function only counts cells with numbers. If you want the Count feature on the status bar to count cells that contain numbers only, right-click anywhere on the status bar > uncheck "Count" and check "Numerical Count" in the Customize Status Bar.

Customize Status Bar

✓	Cell Mode	Ready
✓	Signatures	Off
✓	Information Management Policy	Off
✓	Permissions	Off
	Caps Lock	Off
	Num Lock	Off
✓	Scroll Lock	Off
✓	Fixed Decimal	Off
	Overtype Mode	
✓	End Mode	
	Macro Recording	Not Recording
✓	Selection Mode	
✓	Page Number	
✓	Average	
✓	Count ◄——— Deselect "Count"	
	Numerical Count	
	Minimum	Select
	Maximum	"Numerical
✓	Sum	Count"

This way, only cells with figures within will be displayed on the status bar when a range of cells are highlighted. For instance, when we highlight the "Social Security" column of our payroll, we get a Numerical count on the status bar.

		Payroll		
Last Name	**Social Security Number**	**Date of Employment**	**Hour**	**R**
Spencer	450012432	1/22/2019	50	
Bolt	341112434	7/24/2019	50	
Phrase	670022435	2/24/2018	52	
Miles	882012539	6/3/2017		
Cliton	553112632	12/28/2019		
Simpson	125512442	1/5/2017	45	
Kelly	5220012489	8/23/2019	45	
April	538012498	8/13/2018		
Kinsley	587012489	9/27/2018	30	
Hume	480026440	10/7/2019	30	
Jason	552812450	8/30/2019	30	

Average: 945423752.7   Numerical Count: 11   Sum: 10399661280

But when we highlighted the column for "Last Name" or "First name," nothing showed up in the status bar for Numerical count because they don't contain numerical data.

41

You can carry out a COUNT function for more than one row or column by separating the cell ranges with a comma. For instance, if we wish to carry out a Count function on the Hour and Gross columns in our example (Midas Concept LLC Payroll), we can use the general formula =COUNT(First cell in the range for the Hour Column:Last cell in the range for the Hour Column, First cell in the range for Gross Column:Last cell in the range for the Gross Column). We simply type it thus;

$$=COUNT(F5:F15,H5:H15).$$

Now, let's carry this action out on our Spreadsheet.

	D	E	F	G	H	I	J	K	L	M
	SUM	▾ ✗ ✓ *fx* =COUNT(F5:F15,H5:H15)								
1										
2		**Midas Concept LLC**								
3		Payroll								
4	Social Security Number	Date of Employment	Hour	Rate	Gross					
5	450012432	1/22/2019	50	$75.00	$3,000.00		Count (count up all cells with a #)			
6	341112434	7/24/2019	50	$44.30	$1,772.00		=COUNT(F5:F15,H5:H15)			
7	670022435	2/24/2018	52	$19.90	$835.00					
8	882012539	6/3/2017		$15.00	$0.00					
9	553112632	12/28/2019		$55.50	$0.00		CountA (counts cells that are NOT empty)			
10	125512442	1/5/2017	45	$12.00	$430.00					
11	5220012489	8/23/2019	45	$12.00	$430.00					
12	538012498	8/13/2018		$15.50	$0.00					
13	587012489	9/27/2018	30	$49.00	$1,960.00					
14	480026440	10/7/2019	30	$55.95	$1,808.00					
15	552812450	8/30/2019	30	$45.20	$1,920					

When we hit the ENTER key on the keyboard, it returns 19. Meaning both columns have 19 cells filled with numbers.

	Midas Concept LLC					
	Payroll					
	Date of Employment	Hour	Rate	Gross		
132	1/22/2019	50	$75.00	$3,000.00	Count (count up all cells with a #)	
134	7/24/2019	50	$44.30	$1,772.00	19	
135	2/24/2018	52	$19.90	$835.00		
539	6/3/2017		$15.00	$0.00		
532	12/28/2019		$55.50	$0.00	CountA (counts cells that are NOT empty)	
142	1/5/2017	45	$12.00	$430.00		
189	8/23/2019	45	$12.00	$430.00		
198	8/13/2018		$15.50	$0.00		
189	9/27/2018	30	$49.00	$1,960.00		
140	10/7/2019	30	$55.95	$1,808.00		
150	8/30/2019	30	$45.20	$1,920		

42

COUNTA

The COUNTA function will count the number of cells in a range that are not empty. It counts any data (both text, figures, etc.). Let's assume we have some employees on our payroll without social security numbers, and we want to find out those that have. We can use the COUNTA function to achieve that. Below is the general syntax for the COUNTA Function.

=COUNTA (first cell in range:last cell in range)

For our Payroll, we use

=COUNTA(D5:D15).

SUM			=COUNTA(D5:D15)								
A	B	C	D	E	F	G	H	I	J	K	L	M

Midas Concept LLC
Payroll

Employee No	First Name	Last Name	Social Security Number	Date of Employment	Hour	Rate	Gross			
2437110	Mark	Spencer	450012432	1/22/2019	50	$75.00	$3,000.00		Count (count up all cells with a #)	
2437111	John	Bolt	341112434	7/24/2019	50	$44.30	$1,772.00		19	
2437112	James	Phrase	670022435	2/24/2018	52	$19.90	$835.00			
2437113	Luther	Miles		6/3/2017		$15.00	$0.00			
2437114	Harry	Cliton	553112632	12/28/2019		$55.50	$0.00		CountA (counts cells that are NOT empty)	
2437115	Belis	Simpson	125512442	1/5/2017	45	$12.00	$430.00			
2437116	Bob	Kelly		8/23/2019	45	$12.00	$430.00		=COUNTA(D5:D15)	
2437117	Martins	April	538012498	8/13/2018		$15.50	$0.00			
2437118	James	Kinsley	587012489	9/27/2018	30	$49.00	$1,960.00			
2437119	Robert	Hume	480026440	10/7/2019	30	$55.95	$1,808.00			
2437120	Harold	Jason	552812450	8/30/2019	30	$45.20	$1,920			

From our illustration, we have nine (9) employees out of eleven (11) employees with social security number on the payroll.

Midas Concept LLC
Payroll

mber	Date of Employment	Hour	Rate	Gross		
012432	1/22/2019	50	$75.00	$3,000.00		Count (count up all cells with a #)
112434	7/24/2019	50	$44.30	$1,772.00		19
022435	2/24/2018	52	$19.90	$835.00		
	6/3/2017		$15.00	$0.00		
112632	12/28/2019		$55.50	$0.00		CountA (counts cells that are NOT empty)
512442	1/5/2017	45	$12.00	$430.00		
	8/23/2019	45	$12.00	$430.00		9
012498	8/13/2018		$15.50	$0.00		
012489	9/27/2018	30	$49.00	$1,960.00		
026440	10/7/2019	30	$55.95	$1,808.00		
812450	8/30/2019	30	$45.20	$1,920		

COUNTIF Function

The COUNTIF function counts cells containing numbers in a cell range that meets a particular condition. Note that the COUNTIF function is also used to count cells with dates and text that match specific criteria.

The general syntax for the **COUNTIF** Function is given as

=COUNTIF(range,criteria)

The range represents the set of cells that is to be evaluated. The criteria is the condition in the form of a number, expression, or text that defines which cells will be counted. The criteria can take the form of 40, "40", ">40", "<40", "oranges," etc.

Going back to our example, the Midas Concept LLC Payroll, we want to identify the number of employees earning $12 per hour. Enter the function

=COUNTIF(G:G,"$12")

Where G:G is the column range where the rate per hour for each employee sits, and "$12" is the criteria to meet.

SUM		=COUNTIF(G:G,"$12")									
B	C		D	E	F	G	H	I	J	K	L
26				**Midas Concept LLC**							
27				Payroll							
28 **First Name**	**Last Name**		**Social Security Number**	**Date of Employment**	**Hour**	**Rate**	**Gross**				
29 Mark	Spencer		450012432	1/22/2019	50	$75.00	$3,000.00				
30 John	Bolt		341112434	7/24/2019	50	$44.30	$1,772.00				
31 James	Phrase		670022435	2/24/2018	52	$19.90	$835.00				
32 Luther	Miles		882012539	6/3/2017		$15.00	$0.00	=COUNTIF(G:G,"$12")			
33 Harry	Cliton		553112632	12/28/2019		$55.50	$0.00				
34 Bells	Simpson		125512442	1/5/2017	45	$12.00	$430.00				
35 Bob	Kelly		522001248	8/23/2019	45	$12.00	$430.00				
36 Martins	April		538012498	8/13/2018		$15.50	$0.00				
37 James	Kingsley		587012489	9/27/2018	30	$49.00	$1,960.00				
38 Robert	Hume		480026440	10/7/2019	30	$55.95	$1,808.00				
39 Harold	Jason		552812450	8/30/2019	30	$45.20	$1,920				
40 David	Kessington		421596508	2/11/2019	25	$33.16	$1,025.85				
41 Davis	Gray		207843531	3/27/2017	30	$32.64	$1,012.66				
42 Benjamin	Samuel		317960683	5/7/2018	25	$32.12	$999.47				
43 Anderson	Smith		527728054	2/21/2018	45	$31.59	$986.28				

From our example, the total number of employees earning $12 per hour is 4.

COUNTIFS Function

The COUNTIFS function counts the number of cells in a range that meets multiple criteria (conditions). An essential aspect of the COUNTIFS function is that it can be used as a worksheet function. What this means is that the COUNTIFS function can be entered as part of a formula in a cell of a worksheet.

The syntax for the COUNTIFS function is given thus;

=COUNTIFS(criteria_range1,criteria1,criteria_range2,criteria2)

The **Criteria_range** is the number of cells you wish to evaluate while criteria is the condition(s) in the form of a number, expression, or text that defines which cells will be counted. Criteria are express as 40, "40", ">40", "<40", "oranges,"etc.

We can use the **COUNTIFS function** to identify number of employees who have worked for 50 hours and earn $1772.00.

For the first COUNTIFS criteria we want to ascertain the employees that worked for 52 hours.

While the second criteria is to count employees who earned $1772.00.

=COUNTIFS(F:F,50,H:H,1772.00)

SUM		=COUNTIFS(F:F,50,H:H,1772.00)					

Midas Concept LLC
Payroll

First Name	Last Name	Social Security Number	Date of Employment	Hour	Rate	Gross	
Mark	Spencer	450012432	1/22/2019	50	$75.00	$3,000.00	
John	Bolt	341112434	7/24/2019	50	$44.30	$1,772.00	
James	Phrase	670022435	2/24/2018	52	$19.90	$835.00	
Luther	Miles	882012539	6/3/2017		$15.00	$0.00	
Harry	Cliton	553112632	12/28/2019		$55.50	$0.00	=COUNTIFS(F:F,50,H:H, 1772.00)
Bells	Simpson	125512442	1/5/2017	45	$12.00	$430.00	
Bob	Kelly	522001248	8/23/2018	45	$12.00	$430.00	
Martins	April	538012498	8/13/2018		$15.50	$0.00	
James	Kingsley	587012489	9/27/2018	30	$49.00	$1,960.00	
Robert	Hume	480026440	10/7/2019	30	$55.95	$1,808.00	
Harold	Jason	552812450	8/30/2019	30	$45.20	$1,920	
David	Kessington	421596508	2/11/2019	25	$33.16	$1,025.85	
Davis	Gray	207843531	3/27/2017	30	$32.64	$1,012.66	
Benjamin	Samuel	317960683	5/7/2018	25	$32.12	$999.47	
Anderson	Smith	527728054	2/21/2018	45	$31.59	$986.28	

Our answer is 2. Two employees worked for 52 hours and earned $1772.00

COUNTBLANK Function

The **COUNTBLANK** Function is used to count blank or empty cells in a data sheet. The general syntax is

=COUNTBLANK(range)

For instance in you wish to count the blank cells in a column (e.g. Column J, we write the **COUNTBLANK** function thus

=COUNTBLANK(J:J)

You can also use the **COUNTBLANK** function to count empty cells in an entire table by selecting the entire table. E.g.

=COUNTBLANK(Table1).

MIN & MAX Function

The **MIN Function** talks about the lowest in a range of numbers. It ignores logical values and texts.

Let's look at the Min function for the sales in January from our Sales Spreadsheet. You will observe that it was easy to identify the lowest number within the cell range at a glance. This is easy because the sales report for January is a small data. This process becomes difficult to identify at a glance when a huge range or an extensive datasheet is involved.

The formula to find out the cell holding the minimum value in column C in the example below is given as

=MIN(C8:C11)

	A	B	C	D	E	F	G	H	I	J
1	Sales Spread sheet									
2	5/15/2020									
3										
4						Commission:		8%		
5										
6		Employee ID	January	February	March	April		Total	Average	
7										
8		2437661	10110.25	11175.65	34140.96	15135.15		70562.01	17640.5	
9		2437662	22200.75	12210.63	21240.82	17205.79		72857.99	18214.5	
10		2347663	19210.34	15185.11	25195.14	12310.44		71901.03	17975.26	
11		2437664	35220.15	11195.37	30185.66	19250.14		95851.32	23962.83	
12										
13		Month Total	86741.49	49766.76	110762.6	63901.52				
14		Month Average	21685.37	12441.69	27690.65	15975.38				
15										
16		Lowest (MIN)	←							
17		Highest (MAX)								
18										

Enter the formula and hit the ENTER key on the keyboard to insert the Minimum value in the range of cells. You can get that of February, March and April by copying and pasting the MIN function value of January in that of February to April. Alternatively, you can click and drag the autofill handle across Row 13 above to copy the formula in Cell C13 into Cell D13, E13 and F13.

SUM   × ✓ fx =MIN(C8:C11)

	A	B	C	D	E	F	G	H	I	J
			MIN(number1, [number2], ...)							
1	Sales Spread sheet									
2	5/15/2020									
3										
4						Commission:		8%		
5										
6		Employee ID	January	February	March	April		Total	Average	
7										
8		2437661	10110.25	11175.65	34140.96	15135.15		70562.01	17640.5	
9		2437662	22200.75	12210.63	21240.82	17205.79		72857.99	18214.5	
10		2347663	19210.34	15185.11	25195.14	12310.44		71901.03	17975.26	
11		2437664	35220.15	11195.37	30185.66	19250.14		95851.32	23962.83	
12										
13		Month Total	86741.49	49766.76	110762.6	63901.52				
14		Month Average	21685.37	12441.69	27690.65	15975.38				
15										
16		Lowest (MIN)	=MIN(C8:C11) ←							
17		Highest (MAX)								
18										

	M24			f_x							
	A	B	C	D	E	F	G	H	I	J	K
1	Sales Spread sheet										
2	5/15/2020										
3											
4						Commission:		8%			
5											
6		Employee ID	January	February	March	April		Total	Average		
7											
8		2437661	10110.25	11175.65	34140.96	15135.15		70562.01	17640.5		
9		2437662	22200.75	12210.63	21240.82	17205.79		72857.99	18214.5		
10		2347663	19210.34	15185.11	25195.14	12310.44		71901.03	17975.26		
11		2437664	35220.15	11195.37	30185.66	19250.14		95851.32	23962.83		
12											
13		Month Total	86741.49	49766.76	110762.6	63901.52					
14		Month Average	21685.37	12441.69	27690.65	15975.38					
15											
16		Lowest (MIN)	10110.25	11175.65	21240.82	12310.44					
17		Highest (MAX)									
18											
19											

The maximum function indicates the largest value in a set of values. For the **MAX Function,** the general syntax is given as;

=MAX(First cell in the range:Last cell in the range)

To obtain the maximum value for January in our example, we use the formula

=MAX(C8:C11) as shown below;

	SUM			X ✔ f_x	=MAX(C8:C11)				
	A	B	C	D	E	F	G	H	I
1	Sales Spread sheet								
2	5/15/2020								
3									
4						Commission:		8%	
5									
6		Employee ID	January	February	March	April		Total	Average
7									
8		2437661	10110.25	11175.65	34140.96	15135.15		70562.01	17640.5
9		2437662	22200.75	12210.63	21240.82	17205.79		72857.99	18214.5
10		2347663	19210.34	15185.11	25195.14	12310.44		71901.03	17975.26
11		2437664	35220.15	11195.37	30185.66	19250.14		95851.32	23962.83
12									
13		Month Total	86741.49	49766.76	110762.6	63901.52			
14		Month Average	21685.37	12441.69	27690.65	15975.38			
15									
16		Lowest (MIN)	10110.25	11175.65	21240.82	12310.44			
17		Highest (MAX)	=MAX(C8:C11)						
18									

You can copy the content of the first calculated cell and paste it in the other cells to get the Maximum values for each of the cells. Like the Min function, the Max function ignores logical values and text.

	A	B	C	D	E	F	G	H	I	J
	H22			fx						
1	Sales Spread sheet									
2	5/15/2020									
3										
4						Commission:		8%		
5										
6		Employee ID	January	February	March	April		Total	Average	
7										
8		2437661	10110.25	11175.65	34140.96	15135.15		70562.01	17640.5	
9		2437662	22200.75	12210.63	21240.82	17205.79		72857.99	18214.5	
10		2347663	19210.34	15185.11	25195.14	12310.44		71901.03	17975.26	
11		2437664	35220.15	11195.37	30185.66	19250.14		95851.32	23962.83	
12										
13		Month Total	86741.49	49766.76	110762.6	63901.52				
14		Month Average	21685.37	12441.69	27690.65	15975.38				
15										
16		Lowest (MIN)	10110.25	11175.65	21240.82	12310.44				
17		Highest (MAX)	35220.15	15185.11	34140.96	19250.14				
18				MAX Function						
19										

ROUND Function

ROUND function rounds the decimal places of the number by a specified number. We will look at three Rounds functions in this section, they include Round, Roundup and Rounddown.

The syntax for the Round function is given thus;

$$=Round(argument1, num\_digits)$$

Where **argument1** is the cell or range of cells to be rounded, **num_digits** is the number of decimal places you want after the decimal point for the number(s) in the selected cell(s).

To illustrate the Round Function, we will use the example below;

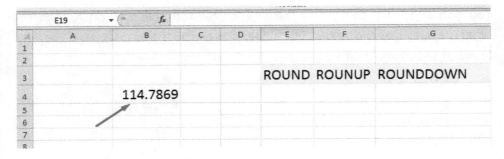

To Round 114.7869 to 2 decimal points, we use the formula

=ROUND(B4,2)

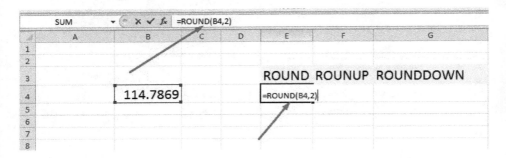

And the answer is given below;

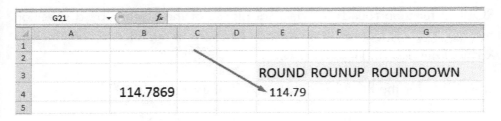

Now, let's round 114.7869 to one decimal point.

We use the formula =**ROUND(B4,1)**

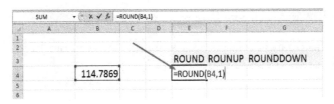

The answer is 114.8

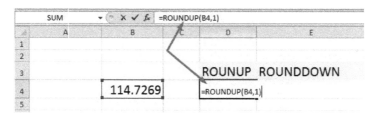

ROUNDUP Function

The Roundup function always rounds a number up away from zero (0).

The syntax for Roundup is similar to that of the Round function.

$$=ROUNDUP(argument1, num\_digits)$$

From example, let's to roundup 114.7269 to one decimal point.

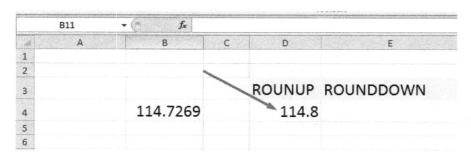

When we Roundup 114.7269 to one decimal point we have 114.8.

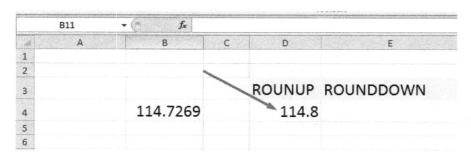

Observe that the number after the decimal point is increased by one irrespective of the fact that the next digit, which is 2, is not up to 5.

ROUNDDOWN Function

The **Rounddown Function** rounds a number down towards zero (O). The general syntax is similar to the Round and Roundup functions.

=ROUNDDOWN(argument1,num_digits)

To illustrate we will ROUNDDOWN 114.7269 to the nearest integer (i.e., O) So the formula will be **=ROUNDUP(B4,0)**.

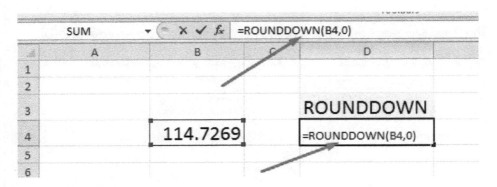

This way, we don't want any number after the decimal point.

When we **ROUNDDOWN** the above example to two decimal places, we get 114.72.

SUM	▾	× ✓ fx	=ROUNDDOWN(B4,2)	
▲	A	B	C	D
1				
2				
3				ROUNDDOWN
4		114.7269		=ROUNDDOWN(B4,2)
5				ROUNDDOWN(number, num_digits)
6				

Note that although the next number after 2 is 6, in **ROUNDDOWN** Function, we do not add 1 to make it 3.

	D5	▾	fx	
▲	A	B	C	D
1				
2				
3				ROUNDDOWN
4		114.7269		114.72

CONCATENATE Function

A **Concatenate Function** joins a list or range of strings. That is, it joins text from two different cells. For instance, if we have the first name and last name in two different cells, we can bring them together in one cell with the aid of the concatenate function. The general syntax for concatenate function is:

=CONCATENATE(argument1,argument2,argument3,…)

Let's concatenate the Last Name and the First Name in the example below.

	D19	▼	f_x	
	A	B	C	D
1				
2		LAST NAME	FIRST NAME	CONCATENATE
3		Ben	Smith	
4		Steve	Cole	
5		Bob	William	
6		McSmith	Gilbert	
7		John	Mills	
8		Harold	Jason	
9		Isaac	Edward	
10		Luky	James	
11		Smith	Harry	
12		Carl	Marx	

To Concatenate the names in the first row, we type in;

=CONCATENATE(B3,C2)

	SUM	▼ X ✔ f_x	=CONCATENATE(B3,C3)		
	A	B	C	D	E
1					
2		LAST NAME	FIRST NAME	CONCATENATE	
3		Ben	Smith	=CONCATENATE(B3,C3)	
4		Steve	Cole		
5		Bob	William		
6		McSmith	Gilbert		
7		John	Mills		
8		Harold	Jason		
9		Isaac	Edward		
10		Luky	James		
11		Smith	Harry		
12		Carl	Marx		

This will bring Ben and Smith together in a cell

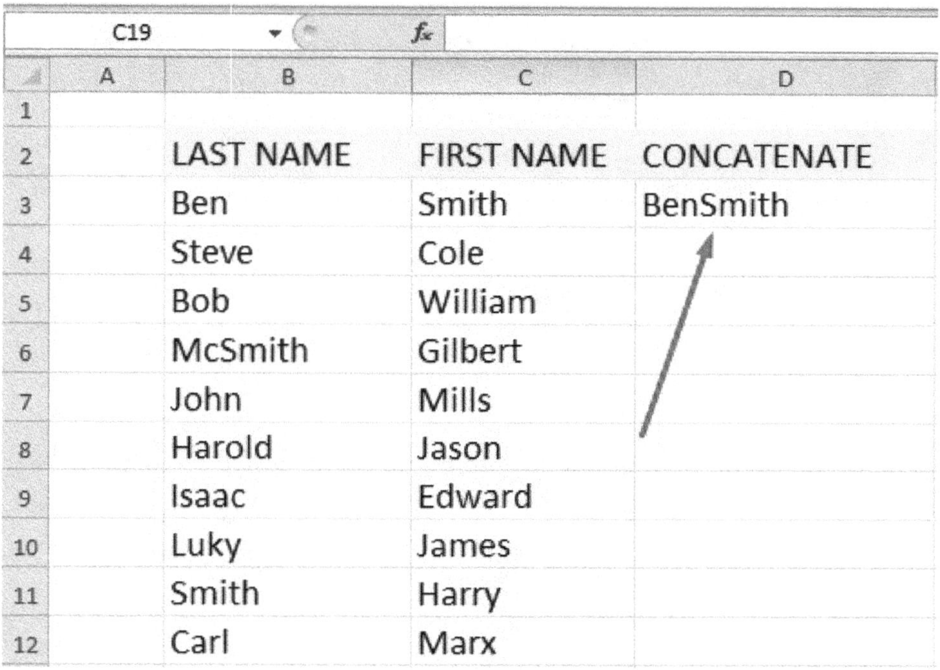

	A	B	C	D
1				
2		LAST NAME	FIRST NAME	CONCATENATE
3		Ben	Smith	BenSmith
4		Steve	Cole	
5		Bob	William	
6		McSmith	Gilbert	
7		John	Mills	
8		Harold	Jason	
9		Isaac	Edward	
10		Luky	James	
11		Smith	Harry	
12		Carl	Marx	

But Note that there is no space between the concatenated names. To add space between concatenated text, we will add space after the comma in the formula before typing the next cel reference. That is

=CONCATENATE(B3, C3)
Space

Now, recall that Excel only recognizes formulas, numbers, Boolean functions (true or false) and cell references, so for it to recognize a space, we must put the space in double-quotes" " followed by a comma before adding the next cell reference.

So, our formula will be

=CONCATENATE(B3, " ",C3)

and hit the ENTER Key on the keyboard

SUM	▾	× ✓ ƒx	=CONCATENATE(B3," ",C3)		
	A	B	C	D	E	F
1						
2		LAST NAME	FIRST NAME	CONCATENATE		
3		Ben	Smith	=CONCATENATE(B3," ",C3)		
4		Steve	Cole			
5		Bob	William			
6		McSmith	Gilbert			
7		John	Mills			
8		Harold	Jason			
9		Isaac	Edward	Space in double quotes and seperated by comma		
10		Luky	James			
11		Smith	Harry			
12		Carl	Marx			

This now concatenates the content of B3 with that of C3 in another cell D3, with space in between the two concatenated text as shown below;

F11	▾	ƒx		
	A	B	C	D
1				
2		LAST NAME	FIRST NAME	CONCATENATE
3		Ben	Smith	Ben Smith
4		Steve	Cole	
5		Bob	William	
6		McSmith	Gilbert	
7		John	Mills	
8		Harold	Jason	
9		Isaac	Edward	
10		Luky	James	
11		Smith	Harry	
12		Carl	Marx	

We can copy this function to the other cells by simply using the fill handle. We highlight the cell with the concatenated text, hover the cursor across the autofill handle until the cursor turns to a black cross, then drag the fill handle down until contents of the other cells are concatenated as well.

	A	B	C	D	E
1					
2		LAST NAME	FIRST NAME	CONCATENATE	Click Drag Down
3		Ben	Smith	Ben Smith	
4		Steve	Cole		
5		Bob	William		
6		McSmith	Gilbert		
7		John	Mills	Fill Handle	
8		Harold	Jason		
9		Isaac	Edward		
10		Luky	James		
11		Smith	Harry		
12		Carl	Marx		
13					

D3 · fx =CONCATENATE(B3," ",C3)

	A	B	C	D
1				
2		LAST NAME	FIRST NAME	CONCATENATE
3		Ben	Smith	Ben Smith
4		Steve	Cole	Steve Cole
5		Bob	William	Bob William
6		McSmith	Gilbert	McSmith Gilbert
7		John	Mills	John Mills
8		Harold	Jason	Harold Jason
9		Isaac	Edward	Isaac Edward
10		Luky	James	Luky James
11		Smith	Harry	Smith Harry
12		Carl	Marx	Carl Marx

Alternatively, to apply the concatenate function to the other cells, hover your cursor on the autofill Handle until it turns to a black cross, then double-click.

INDEX Function

The Index function returns the value or reference of the cell at the intersection of a particular row and column in the given range.

The general syntax for the index function is

=INDEX(range1,row number,column number)

Supposing you have a list of orders and their unit price like in the example below,

	A	B	C	D
1	**Order ID**	**Product**	**Unit Price**	**Quantity**
2	23412	Eggs	$14.00	10
3	23413	Carrots	$9.90	12
4	23414	Oranges	$14.90	9
5	23415	Mangoes	$17.60	5
6	23416	Grapes	$40.20	30
7	23417	Pears	$26.50	35

We can use the index formula to look up the quantity of oranges sold and here is how to do that. In the cell where you want the result, type in the index function. The first requirement for the index function is the array. The array here is the table where you are extracting the data from, so we highlight the entire table to get the cell reference for the array. Next, we need the row number (the row where orange sits). Next, we get the column we are to derive the result from, and in our example, it is the 'Quantity' Column. Then close the bracket and press the ENTER key on your keyboard to get the answer. Now, let's write the formula using our example

=INDEX(A1:D7,4,4)

Where A1:D7 is the array. Which is the cell reference of the entire table in our illustration

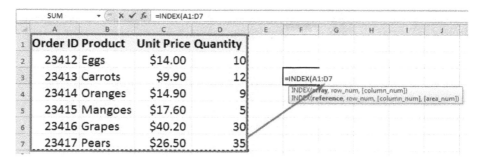

	A	B	C	D
1	Order ID	Product	Unit Price	Quantity
2	23412	Eggs	$14.00	10
3	23413	Carrots	$9.90	12
4	23414	Oranges	$14.90	9
5	23415	Mangoes	$17.60	5
6	23416	Grapes	$40.20	30
7	23417	Pears	$26.50	35

`=INDEX(A1:D7`

INDEX(array, row_num, [column_num])
INDEX(reference, row_num, [column_num], [area_num])

The first 4 is the row number where oranges sit

	A	B	C	D
1	Order ID	Product	Unit Price	Quantity
2	23412	Eggs	$14.00	10
3	23413	Carrots	$9.90	12
4	23414	Oranges	$14.90	9
5	23415	Mangoes	$17.60	5
6	23416	Grapes	$40.20	30
7	23417	Pears	$26.50	35

And the second 4 in the formula is the column number where the result is to be extracted from.

SUM   X ✓ fx   =INDEX(A1:D7,4,4)

	A	B	C	D	E	F	G
1	Order ID	Product	Unit Price	Quantity			
2	23412	Eggs	$14.00	10		INDEX	
3	23413	Carrots	$9.90	12		=INDEX(A1:D7,4,4)	
4	23414	Oranges	$14.90	9			
5	23415	Mangoes	$17.60	5			
6	23416	Grapes	$40.20	30			
7	23417	Pears	$26.50	35			

When we hit the ENTER key on the keyboard, we got nine (9) as our result, which is the quantity of orange ordered.

	A	B	C	D	E	F
1	**Order ID**	**Product**	**Unit Price**	**Quantity**		
2	23412	Eggs	$14.00	10		INDEX
3	23413	Carrots	$9.90	12		9
4	23414	Oranges	$14.90	9		
5	23415	Mangoes	$17.60	5		
6	23416	Grapes	$40.20	30		
7	23417	Pears	$26.50	35		

Exercise:

Use the index function to find out the quantity of Grapes ordered.

OFFSET Function

The Excel OFFSET function returns a reference to a range that is a given number of rows and columns from a given reference. The general syntax for the OFFSET function is given thus;

=OFFSET(offset, row number, column number, [height], [width])

*Height and Width, although optional, are used for calculating offset. Let's do some illustration with the product order worksheet below

	A	B	C	D
1	**Order ID**	**Product**	**Unit Price**	**Quantity**
2	23412	Eggs	$14.00	10
3	23413	Carrots	$9.90	12
4	23414	Oranges	$14.90	9
5	23415	Mangoes	$17.60	5
6	23416	Grapes	$40.20	30
7	23417	Pears	$26.50	35

We can get the quantity ordered using our OFFSET Function

However, unlike the INDEX function, we do not have arrays in the OFFSET syntax. We only have the Cell reference, which is the first cell (Cell A1), the row number is the row after the reference cell (i.e., Row 2), and Column number is the Column where the target cell is. (in this case, column 3).

So to get the quantity of oranges ordered using the OFFSET Function we write the formula thus;

$$=OFFSET(A1,3,3)$$

The A1 represents the first cell

	A	B	C	D
1	**Order ID**	**Product**	**Unit Price**	**Quantity**
2	23412	Eggs	$14.00	10
3	23413	Carrots	$9.90	12
4	23414	Oranges	$14.90	9
5	23415	Mangoes	$17.60	5
6	23416	Grapes	$40.20	30
7	23417	Pears	$26.50	35
8				
9			Reference Cell	
10			(A1)	
11				
12				

The first three (3) after A1 represents the row number where 'oranges' sit. We count from top top-down starting from the row after the offset.

⊿	A	B	C	D	E
1	**Order ID**	**Product**	**Unit Price**	**Quantity**	
Row 1 / 2	23412	Eggs	$14.00	10	
Row 2 / 3	23413	Carrots	$9.90	12	
Row 3 / 4	23414	Oranges	$14.90	9	
5	23415	Mangoes	$17.60	5	
6	23416	Grapes	$40.20	30	
7	23417	Pears	$26.50	35	
8					
9				Offset	

The second three (3) represents the target column number after the offset. The target cell is on Column 3, counting from left to right, beginning from the column after the offset column.

⊿	A	Column 1	Column 2	Column 3	E
1	**Order ID**	**Product**	**Unit Price**	**Quantity**	
2	23412	Eggs	$14.00	10	
3	23413	Carrots	$9.90	12	
4	23414	Oranges	$14.90	9	
5	23415	Mangoes	$17.60	5	
6	23416	Grapes	$40.20	30	
7	23417	Pears	$26.50	35	
8					
9		Offset			
10					

So, after typing in the formula =**OFFSET(A1,3,3)**

	A	B	C	D	E	F	G
SUM	▾ ⊙ ✗ ✓ ƒx	=OFFSET(A1,3,)					
1	Order ID	Product	Unit Price	Quantity			
2	23412	Eggs	$14.00	10		INDEX	OFFSET
3	23413	Carrots	$9.90	12		9	=OFFSET(A1,3,)
4	23414	Oranges	$14.90	9			
5	23415	Mangoes	$17.60	5			
6	23416	Grapes	$40.20	30			
7	23417	Pears	$26.50	35			

We get the quantity of oranges ordered.

	A	B	C	D	E	F	G
1	Order ID	Product	Unit Price	Quantity			
2	23412	Eggs	$14.00	10		INDEX	OFFSET
3	23413	Carrots	$9.90	12		9	9
4	23414	Oranges	$14.90	9			
5	23415	Mangoes	$17.60	5			
6	23416	Grapes	$40.20	30			
7	23417	Pears	$26.50	35			
8							
9							
10							

Let's see an example of an OFFSET Function that requires 'Height' and 'Width'. Below is a Midas Sales report for two cities Texas and New York

	A	B	C	D	E
1		**Midas Sales Report for Two Cities**			
2	**Month**	**Texas**	**New York**		
3	Jan	510	1010		
4	Feb	600	1468		
5	Mar	645	1035		
6	Apr	156	1031		
7	May	692	589		
8	Jun	862	695		
9	Jul	380	1220		
10	Aug	388	611		
11	Sep	930	1160		
12	Oct	341	747		
13	Nov	645	1214		
14	Dec	935	1210		

'Height' and 'width' are useful when using the OFFSET function with any other function. For instance, if you are using the OFFSET function with the SUM function, then the Height and Width become useful, for example. Let's say we are looking for the sum of February to May for sales in Texas and New York together. To do this, we use the SUM Function and the OFFSET function together

$$=SUM(OFFSET(A2,2,1,4,2))$$

OFFSET(offset, row number, column number, [height], [width])

Where A2 is the Offset

	A	B	C	D	E
1		**Midas Sales Report for Two Cities**			
2	**Month**	**Texas**	**New York**		
3	Jan	510	1010		
4	Feb	600	1468		
5	Mar	645	1035		
6	Apr	156	1031		
7	May	692	589		
8	Jun	862	695		
9	Jul	380	1220		
10	Aug	388	611		
11	Sep	930	1160	Offset Cell A2	
12	Oct	341	747		
13	Nov	645	1214		
14	Dec	935	1210		

The '2' refers to the row number we are starting our addition from (i.e., February) and February is in the second row after the offset, hence the number 2.

A	B	C	D
1	**Midas Sales Report for Two Cities**		
2 **Month**	**Texas**	**New York**	
3 Jan	510	1010	
4 Feb	600	1468	
5 Mar	645	1035	
6 Apr	156	1031	
7 May	692	589	
8 Jun	862	695	Row nuber 2 after the offset
9 Jul	380	1220	
10 Aug	388	611	
11 Sep	930	1160	
12 Oct	341	747	
13 Nov	645	1214	
14 Dec	935	1210	

The column number is '1'. This indicates that the target Months (Feb, Mar, Apr and May) sits in Column 1. The height is 4. This means the number of rows from February to May is 4, which represents the height.

A	B	C	D	E
1	**Midas Sales Report for Two Cities**			
2 **Month**	**Texas**	**New York**		
3 Jan	510	1010		
4 Feb	600	1468		
5 Mar	645	1035	Height 4 Rows	
6 Apr	156	1031		
7 May	692	589		
8 Jun	862	695		
9 Jul	380	1220		
10 Aug	388	611		
11 Sep	930	1160		
12 Oct	341	747		
13 Nov	645	1214		
14 Dec	935	1210		

The width is 2. This means the content of the cells that need to be added occupies only two columns.

	A	B	C	D	E
1		**Midas Sales Report for Two Cities**			
2	**Month**	**Texas**	**New York**		
3	Jan	510	1010		
4	Feb	600	1468		
5	Mar	645	1035		
6	Apr	156	1031		
7	May	692	589		
8	Jun	862	695		
9	Jul	380	1220		
10	Aug	388	611		
11	Sep	930	1160		
12	Oct	341	747		Width is in 2 Columns
13	Nov	645	1214		
14	Dec	935	1210		
15					

So we have =**SUM(OFFSET(A2,2,1,4,2))**

				=SUM(OFFSET(A2,2,1,4,2))				
SUM								
	A	B	C	D	E	F	G	H
1		**Midas Sales Report for Two Cities**						
2	**Month**	Texas	New York				OFFSET	
3	Jan	510	1010				=SUM(OFFSET(A2,2,1,4,2))	
4	Feb	600	1468					
5	Mar	645	1035					
6	Apr	156	1031					
7	May	692	589					
8	Jun	862	695					
9	Jul	380	1220					
10	Aug	388	611					
11	Sep	930	1160					
12	Oct	341	747					
13	Nov	645	1214					
14	Dec	935	1210					

And when we press the ENTER key on the keyword after closing the bracket in the formula, we get 6216.

	A	B	C	D	E	F
1		**Midas Sales Report for Two Cities**				
2	**Month**	**Texas**	**New York**			**OFFSET**
3	Jan	510	1010			6216
4	Feb	600	1468			
5	Mar	645	1035			
6	Apr	156	1031			
7	May	692	589			
8	Jun	862	695			
9	Jul	380	1220			
10	Aug	388	611			
11	Sep	930	1160			
12	Oct	341	747			
13	Nov	645	1214			
14	Dec	935	1210			

Several functions can be combined with the OFFSET Function. For instance, Average Function, Product Function, Count Function, and so on.

MATCH Function

The Excel MATCH Function returns the relative position of an item in an array that matches a specific value in a specified order. In other words, it searches for a specified item in a range of cells and returns the relative position of that item in the range. The general syntax for the Match function is;

=MATCH(lookup value, lookup array, match type)

However, the Lookup value can be a number or text, while the lookup range is the range of selected cells. Finally, the match type can be Greater Than, Exact March or Less Than represented by 1, 0, or -1, respectively.

	A	B	C	D
1	**Order ID**	**Product**	**Unit Price**	**Quantity**
2	23412	Eggs	$14.00	10
3	23413	Carrots	$9.90	12
4	23414	Oranges	$14.90	9
5	23415	Mangoes	$17.60	5
6	23416	Grapes	$40.20	30
7	23417	Pears	$26.50	35

Sticking with our product order worksheet example, let's use the Match Function to figure out what row 'oranges' sits. In this case, the MATCH Function will identify what row the product 'Oranges' sits. Our lookup value is "Oranges." For the array row, select all the products column, including the header (B:B). Match type could be greater than (1), Exact match (0) or less than (-1). For our example, we are looking for the exact match, so we select zero (0). To write the formula, we have

$$=MATCH("Oranges",B:B,0)$$

This is expressed in our worksheet as:

SUM		× ✓ ƒx	=MATCH("Oranges",B:B,0)							
	A	B	C	D	E	F	G	H	I	J
1	Order ID	Product	Unit Price	Quantity						
2	23412	Eggs	$14.00	10		INDEX	OFFSET	MATCH		
3	23413	Carrots	$9.90	12		9	9	=MATCH("Oranges",B:B,0)		
4	23414	Oranges	$14.90	9						
5	23415	Mangoes	$17.60	5						
6	23416	Grapes	$40.20	30						
7	23417	Pears	$26.50	35						
8										
9										

And when we hit the ENTER key on the keyboard, we get 4 as the answer. This means 'Oranges' sits on Row 4 in our worksheet.

	A	B	C	D	E	F	G	H
1	**Order ID**	**Product**	**Unit Price**	**Quantity**				
2	23412	Eggs	$14.00	10		INDEX	OFFSET	MATCH
3	23413	Carrots	$9.90	12		9	9	4
4	23414	Oranges	$14.90	9				
5	23415	Mangoes	$17.60	5				
6	23416	Grapes	$40.20	30				
7	23417	Pears	$26.50	35				

Exercise: Use the MATCH function to look for the exact row 'Mangoes' sit.

Trim Function

The Excel Trim Function eliminates extra spaces from the text string except for the single space between words. In other words, it removes unwanted spaces within a particular cell or range of cells. It will only remove spaces at the front and end of the text, if any. The general syntax for the Trim Function is given as;

$$=TRIM(Cell1)$$

To illustrate how to use the TRIM Function, on the First name Column of our Midas Concept LLC Payroll worksheet, we will add some spaces before and after some names, and used the TRIM function to get rid of those spaces. To do this, we remove the space in the First Cell, which in our illustration, is cell B29. So we say,

$$=TRIM(B29)$$

SUM · × ✓ fx =TRIM(B29)

	C	D	E	F	G	H	I	J	K
26			**Midas Concept LLC**						
27			Payroll						
28	**Last Name**	**Social Security Number**	**Date of Employment**	**Hour**	**Rate**	**Gross**		**TRIM**	
29	Spencer	450012432	1/22/2019	50	$75.00	$3,000.00		=TRIM(B29)	
30	Bolt	341112434	7/24/2019	50	$44.30	$1,772.00			
31	Phrase	670022435	2/24/2018	52	$19.90	$835.00			
32	Miles	882012539	6/3/2017		$15.00	$0.00			
33	Cliton	553112632	12/28/2019		$55.50	$0.00			
34	Simpson	125512442	1/5/2017	45	$12.00	$430.00			
35	Kelly	522001248	8/23/2019	45	$12.00	$430.00			
36	April	538012498	8/13/2018		$15.50	$0.00			
37	Kingsley	587012489	9/27/2018	30	$49.00	$1,960.00			
38	Hume	480026440	10/7/2019	30	$55.95	$1,808.00			

This removes all the extra spaces within Cell B29. Now, to apply this to the names in the entire column (i.e. First Name), we double click on the fill handle or we highlight the cell, hover the cursor on the fill handle until the cross turn dark, then we click and drag it down across the entire column that corresponds to the target column. Now, there are no more spaces at the front and back of the texts. Highlight and Copy the column where the Trimmed names are placed > go back to the original data, right-click on the first cell and click 'Paste Special.' On the 'paste special' window that pops up, select 'Values' and click the "OK" button.

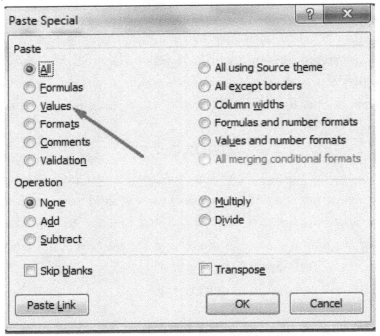

The 'paste special' prevents you from bringing the Trim formulas along with the copied names.

SQRT Function

The SQRT function calculates the square root of the numeric value. The general syntax for SQRT function is

$$=SQRT(cell1)$$

For example, let's find the SQRT of a number 23417 sitting in Cell C14.

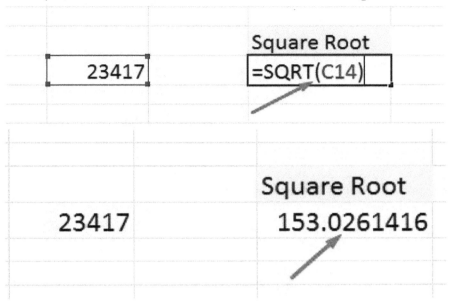

TODAY Function

TODAY function returns the current date. The General Syntax for TODAY function is;

$$=TODAY()$$

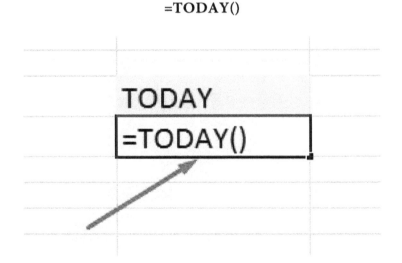

When you hit ENTER key, it returns the current date.

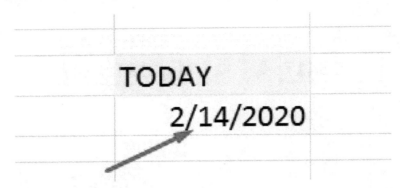

The date returned by 'TODAY Function' is the System or your PC's date. If, by any chance, your System's date is not correct, you will need to fix it to prevent Excel from using a wrong date for the TODAY Function.

Chapter Four
Logical Excel Functions

There are four main logical functions in Excel, IF, AND, OR, and NOT. However, other sub-logical functions are derived from these four, namely XOR, IFERROR, IFNA, and NESTEDIFs.

IF Function

The **IF Function** is one of the most important Logical Excel functions. It checks if a condition is met and returns one value if True and another Value if False.

The general Syntax for the IF Function is given thus;

=IF(Logic, Value if true, Value of False)

We can use the IF function in our Midas Concept LLC Payroll to give $100 commission to employees who have worked up to 58 hours.

				Midas Concept LLC				
				Payroll				
Employee No	First Name	Last Name	Social Security Number	Date of Employment	Hour	Rate	Gross	COMMISSION
b2437110	Mark	Spencer	450012432	1/22/2019	50	$75.00	$3,000.00	
b2437111	John	Bolt	341112434	7/24/2019	50	$44.30	$1,772.00	
a2437112	James	Phrase	670022435	2/24/2018	52	$19.90	$835.00	
b2437113	Luther	Miles	882012539	6/3/2017	58	$15.00	$1,770.00	
2437114	Harry	Cliton	553112632	12/28/2019	58	$55.50	$1,623.00	
2437115	Bells	Simpson	125512442	1/5/2017	45	$12.00	$430.00	
b2437116	Bob	Kelly	522001248	8/23/2019	45	$12.00	$430.00	
b2437117	Martins	April	538012498	8/13/2018	58	$15.50	$1,807.00	
2437118	James	Kingsley	587012489	9/27/2018	58	$49.00	$1,960.00	
2437119	Robert	Hume	480026440	10/7/2019	30	$55.95	$1,808.00	
b2437120	Harold	Jason	552812450	8/30/2019	30	$45.20	$1,920	
b2437121	David	Kessington	421596508	2/11/2019	25	$33.16	$1,025.85	
b2437122	Davis	Gray	207843531	3/27/2017	30	$32.64	$1,012.66	
a2437123	Benjamin	Samuel	317960683	5/7/2018	25	$32.12	$999.47	
b2437124	Anderson	Smith	527728054	2/21/2018	45	$31.59	$986.28	
a2437125	Wright	Clark	200968363	7/17/2017	29	$31.07	$973.09	
a2437126	Mitchell	Johnson	523191905	5/14/2017	32	$30.54	$959.90	
a2437127	Thomas	Rodriguez	213597710	11/24/2016	45	$30.02	$946.71	

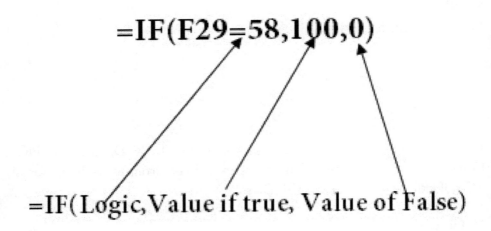

$$=IF(F29=58,100,0)$$

$$=IF(Logic, Value\ if\ true,\ Value\ of\ False)$$

What the above formula simply means is that if the first employee's hour of work is up to 58 (first employee hour of work is located in F29 in our illustration), then give him or her $100 as commission, if the employee hasn't worked for 58 hours, don't give him or her any commission. In other words, zero (0) commission for those who do not qualify.

Employee No	First Name	Last Name	Social Security Number	Date of Employment	Hour	Rate	Gross	COMMISSION
				Midas Concept LLC				
				Payroll				
b2437110	Mark	Spencer	450012432	1/22/2019	50	$75.00	$3,000.00	=IF(F29=58,100,0)
b2437111	John	Bolt	341112434	7/24/2019	50	$44.30	$1,772.00	
a2437112	James	Phrase	670022435	2/24/2018	52	$19.90	$835.00	
b2437113	Luther	Miles	882012539	6/3/2017	58	$15.00	$1,770.00	
2437114	Harry	Cliton	553112632	12/28/2019	58	$55.50	$1,623.00	
2437115	Bells	Simpson	125512442	1/5/2017	45	$12.00	$430.00	
b2437116	Bob	Kelly	522001248	8/23/2019	45	$12.00	$430.00	
b2437117	Martins	April	538012498	8/13/2018	58	$15.50	$1,807.00	
2437118	James	Kingsley	587012489	9/27/2018	58	$49.00	$1,960.00	
2437119	Robert	Hume	480026440	10/7/2019	30	$55.95	$1,808.00	
b2437120	Harold	Jason	552812450	8/30/2019	30	$45.20	$1,920	
b2437121	David	Kessington	421596508	2/11/2019	25	$33.16	$1,025.85	
b2437122	Davis	Gray	207843531	3/27/2017	30	$32.64	$1,012.66	
a2437123	Benjamin	Samuel	317960683	5/7/2018	25	$32.12	$999.47	
b2437124	Anderson	Smith	527728054	2/21/2018	45	$31.59	$986.28	
a2437125	Wright	Clark	200968363	7/17/2017	29	$31.07	$973.09	
a2437126	Mitchell	Johnson	523191905	5/14/2017	32	$30.54	$959.90	

Now, the first employee will return zero, because he has only worked for 50 hours and is not qualified for a $100 commission. Next, hover your cursor over the fill handle and when the black cross appears, double click to apply the same formula to the other employees, and you will see the list of employees that qualified for the $100 commission.

Employee No	First Name	Last Name	Social Security Numbe	Date of Employmei	Hour	Rate	Gross	COMMISSION
			Midas Concept LLC					
				Payroll				
b2437110	Mark	Spencer	450012432	1/22/2019	50	$75.00	$3,000.00	0
b2437111	John	Bolt	341112434	7/24/2019	50	$44.30	$1,772.00	0
a2437112	James	Phrase	670022435	2/24/2018	52	$19.90	$835.00	0
b2437113	Luther	Miles	882012539	6/3/2017	58	$15.00	$1,770.00	100
2437114	Harry	Cliton	553112632	12/28/2019	58	$55.50	$1,623.00	100
2437115	Bells	Simpson	125512442	1/5/2017	45	$12.00	$430.00	0
b2437116	Bob	Kelly	522001248	8/23/2019	45	$12.00	$430.00	0
b2437117	Martins	April	538012498	8/13/2018	58	$15.50	$1,807.00	100
2437118	James	Kingsley	587012489	9/27/2018	58	$49.00	$1,960.00	100
2437119	Robert	Hume	480026440	10/7/2019	30	$55.95	$1,808.00	0
b2437120	Harold	Jason	552812450	8/30/2019	30	$45.20	$1,920	0
b2437121	David	Kessington	421596508	2/11/2019	25	$33.16	$1,025.85	0
b2437122	Davis	Gray	207843531	3/27/2017	30	$32.64	$1,012.66	0
a2437123	Benjamin	Samuel	317960683	5/7/2018	25	$32.12	$999.47	0
b2437124	Anderson	Smith	527728054	2/21/2018	45	$31.59	$986.28	0
a2437125	Wright	Clark	200968363	7/17/2017	29	$31.07	$973.09	0
a2437126	Mitchell	Johnson	523191905	5/14/2017	32	$30.54	$959.90	0

Let's look at another 'IF Function' example. But before we do that, let's add another column to our Midas Concept LLC payroll and that column will hold the department of each employee.

Employee No	First Name	Last Name	SSN	Department	Employment Date	Hour	Rate	Gross	COMMISSION
					Midas Concept LLC				
					Payroll				
b2437110	Mark	Spencer	450012432	Admin	1/22/2019	50	$75.00	$3,000.00	
b2437111	John	Bolt	341112434	Sales	7/24/2019	50	$44.30	$1,772.00	
a2437112	James	Phrase	670022435	Sales	2/24/2018	52	$19.90	$835.00	
b2437113	Luther	Miles	882012539	Marketing	6/3/2017	58	$15.00	$1,770.00	
2437114	Harry	Cliton	553112632	Sales	12/28/2019	58	$55.50	$1,623.00	
2437115	Bells	Simpson	125512442	Personnel	1/5/2017	45	$12.00	$430.00	
b2437116	Bob	Kelly	522001248	Human Resource	8/23/2019	45	$12.00	$430.00	
b2437117	Martins	April	538012498	Sales	8/13/2018	58	$15.50	$1,807.00	
2437118	James	Kingsley	587012489	Admin	9/27/2018	58	$49.00	$1,960.00	
2437119	Robert	Hume	480026440	Sales	10/7/2019	30	$55.95	$1,808.00	
b2437120	Harold	Jason	552812450	Sales	8/30/2019	30	$45.20	$1,920	
b2437121	David	Kessington	421596508	Sales	2/11/2019	25	$33.16	$1,025.85	
b2437122	Davis	Gray	207843531	Marketing	3/27/2017	30	$32.64	$1,012.66	
a2437123	Benjamin	Samuel	317960683	Marketing	5/7/2018	25	$32.12	$999.47	
b2437124	Anderson	Smith	527728054	Sales	2/21/2018	45	$31.59	$986.28	
a2437125	Wright	Clark	200968363	Director	7/17/2017	29	$31.07	$973.09	

In our illustration, let's say management has decided to give every empl-oyee in the sales department $200 for a job well done. We can use the IF Function to execute this.

$$=IF(E29="Sales",200,0)$$

This means if the first employee is in sales, give him or her $200 commission, else don't give him or her any commission (Zero commission).

Midas Concept LLC
Payroll

Employee No	First Name	Last Name	SSN	Department	Employment Date	Hour	Rate	Gross	COMMISSION
b2437110	Mark	Spencer	450012432	Admin	1/22/2019	50	$75.00	$3,000.00	=IF(E29="Sales",200,0)
b2437111	John	Bolt	341112434	Sales	7/24/2019	50	$44.30	$1,772.00	
a2437112	James	Phrase	670022435	Sales	2/24/2018	52	$19.90	$835.00	
b2437113	Luther	Miles	882012539	Marketing	6/3/2017	58	$15.00	$1,770.00	
2437114	Harry	Cliton	553112632	Sales	12/28/2019	58	$55.50	$1,623.00	
2437115	Bells	Simpson	125512442	Personnel	1/5/2017	45	$12.00	$430.00	
b2437116	Bob	Kelly	522001248	Human Resource	8/23/2019	45	$12.00	$430.00	
b2437117	Martins	April	538012498	Sales	8/13/2018	58	$15.50	$1,807.00	
2437118	James	Kingsley	587012489	Admin	9/27/2018	58	$49.00	$1,960.00	
2437119	Robert	Hume	480026440	Sales	10/7/2019	30	$55.95	$1,808.00	
b2437120	Harold	Jason	552812450	Sales	8/30/2019	30	$45.20	$1,920	
b2437121	David	Kessington	421596508	Sales	2/11/2019	25	$33.16	$1,025.85	
b2437122	Davis	Gray	207843531	Marketing	3/27/2017	30	$32.64	$1,012.66	
a2437123	Benjamin	Samuel	317960683	Marketing	5/7/2018	25	$32.12	$999.47	
b2437124	Anderson	Smith	527728054	Sales	2/21/2018	45	$31.59	$986.28	
a2437125	Wright	Clark	200968363	Director	7/17/2017	29	$31.07	$973.09	

We got zero (0) for the first employee because he is in the 'Admin' department and not in 'Sales,' so he is not entitled to the $200 commission. To apply the function to the remaining employee, click on the cell with the first result, hover your cursor over the fill handle until the black cross appears, then double click on it. This automatically allocates $200 to all employees in the 'Sales' department.

Midas Concept LLC
Payroll

Employee No	First Name	Last Name	SSN	Department	Employment Date	Hour	Rate	Gross	COMMISSION
b2437110	Mark	Spencer	450012432	Admin	1/22/2019	50	$75.00	$3,000.00	0
b2437111	John	Bolt	341112434	Sales	7/24/2019	50	$44.30	$1,772.00	200
a2437112	James	Phrase	670022435	Sales	2/24/2018	52	$19.90	$835.00	200
b2437113	Luther	Miles	882012539	Marketing	6/3/2017	58	$15.00	$1,770.00	0
2437114	Harry	Cliton	553112632	Sales	12/28/2019	58	$55.50	$1,623.00	200
2437115	Bells	Simpson	125512442	Personnel	1/5/2017	45	$12.00	$430.00	0
b2437116	Bob	Kelly	522001248	Human Resource	8/23/2019	45	$12.00	$430.00	0
b2437117	Martins	April	538012498	Sales	8/13/2018	58	$15.50	$1,807.00	200
2437118	James	Kingsley	587012489	Admin	9/27/2018	58	$49.00	$1,960.00	0
2437119	Robert	Hume	480026440	Sales	10/7/2019	30	$55.95	$1,808.00	200
b2437120	Harold	Jason	552812450	Sales	8/30/2019	30	$45.20	$1,920	200
b2437121	David	Kessington	421596508	Sales	2/11/2019	25	$33.16	$1,025.85	200
b2437122	Davis	Gray	207843531	Marketing	3/27/2017	30	$32.64	$1,012.66	0
a2437123	Benjamin	Samuel	317960683	Marketing	5/7/2018	25	$32.12	$999.47	0
b2437124	Anderson	Smith	527728054	Sales	2/21/2018	45	$31.59	$986.28	200
a2437125	Wright	Clark	200968363	Director	7/17/2017	29	$31.07	$973.09	0

AND Function

The **AND Function** in Excel checks if all the logical arguments in a function are valid and return it as "True" and "False" if one of them is not Valid.

The general syntax for the **AND Function** is

$$=AND(Logic1, Logic2, Logic3, \ldots)$$

In our example, we will look at employees of Midas Concept LLC who are working in the sales department and have worked for 50 hours. So if an employee is in the sales department and has worked for 50 hours, it will return 'True' else it will return 'False.'

To illustrate this, let's bring up our Midas Concept LLC Payroll

	Midas Concept LLC								
					Payroll				
Employee No	First Name	Last Name	SSN	Department	Employment Date	Hour	Rate	Gross	AND
b2437110	Mark	Spencer	450012432	Admin	1/22/2019	50	$75.00	$3,000.00	
b2437111	John	Bolt	341112434	Sales	7/24/2019	50	$44.30	$1,772.00	
a2437112	James	Phrase	670022435	Sales	2/24/2018	52	$19.90	$835.00	
b2437113	Luther	Miles	882012539	Marketing	6/3/2017	58	$15.00	$1,770.00	
2437114	Harry	Cliton	553112632	Sales	12/28/2019	58	$55.50	$1,623.00	
2437115	Bells	Simpson	125512442	Personnel	1/5/2017	45	$12.00	$430.00	
b2437116	Bob	Kelly	522001248	Human Resource	8/23/2019	45	$12.00	$430.00	
b2437117	Martins	April	538012498	Sales	8/13/2018	58	$15.50	$1,807.00	
2437118	James	Kingsley	587012489	Admin	9/27/2018	58	$49.00	$1,960.00	
2437119	Robert	Hume	480026440	Sales	10/7/2019	30	$55.95	$1,808.00	
b2437120	Harold	Jason	552812450	Sales	8/30/2019	30	$45.20	$1,920	
b2437121	David	Kessington	421596508	Sales	2/11/2019	25	$33.16	$1,025.85	
b2437122	Davis	Gray	207843531	Marketing	3/27/2017	30	$32.64	$1,012.66	
a2437123	Benjamin	Samuel	317960683	Marketing	5/7/2018	25	$32.12	$999.47	
b2437124	Anderson	Smith	527728054	Sales	2/21/2018	45	$31.59	$986.28	
a2437125	Wright	Clark	200968363	Director	7/17/2017	29	$31.07	$973.09	

So let's start with the first employee Mark Spencer. Using the AND Function, we insert the first logical statement is Mark Spencer's Department = "Sales"? Next, we enter the next logical statement for Mark Spencer. Is the Number of Hours worked equal 50? Now let's represent the above statement using the AND Function;

$$=AND(E29="Sales", H29= 50)$$

Now, close the bracket and hit the ENTER key on the keyboard. When we do this on the Excel sheet, we get the result as shown in the screen shot below;

Midas Concept LLC
Payroll

Employee No	First Name	Last Name	SSN	Department	Employment Date	Hour	Rate	Gross	AND
b2437110	Mark	Spencer	450012432	Admin	1/22/2019	50	$75.00	$3,000.00	=AND(E29="Sales",G29=50)
b2437111	John	Bolt	341112434	Sales	7/24/2019	50	$44.30	$1,772.00	
a2437112	James	Phrase	670022435	Sales	2/24/2018	52	$19.90	$835.00	
b2437113	Luther	Miles	882012539	Marketing	6/3/2017	58	$15.00	$1,770.00	
2437114	Harry	Cliton	553112632	Sales	12/28/2019	58	$55.50	$1,623.00	
2437115	Bells	Simpson	125512442	Personnel	1/5/2017	45	$12.00	$430.00	
b2437116	Bob	Kelly	522001248	Human Resource	8/23/2019	45	$12.00	$430.00	
b2437117	Martins	April	538012498	Sales	8/13/2018	58	$15.50	$1,807.00	
2437118	James	Kingsley	587012489	Admin	9/27/2018	58	$49.00	$1,960.00	
2437119	Robert	Hume	480026440	Sales	10/7/2019	30	$55.95	$1,808.00	
b2437120	Harold	Jason	552812450	Sales	8/30/2019	30	$45.20	$1,920	
b2437121	David	Kessington	421596508	Sales	2/11/2019	25	$33.16	$1,025.85	
b2437122	Davis	Gray	207843531	Marketing	3/27/2017	30	$32.64	$1,012.66	
a2437123	Benjamin	Samuel	317960683	Marketing	5/7/2018	25	$32.12	$999.47	
b2437124	Anderson	Smith	527728054	Sales	2/21/2018	45	$31.59	$986.28	
a2437125	Wright	Clark	200968363	Director	7/17/2017	29	$31.07	$973.09	

It returns the result as "False."

Midas Concept LLC
Payroll

Employee No	First Name	Last Name	SSN	Department	Employment Date	Hour	Rate	Gross	AND
b2437110	Mark	Spencer	450012432	Admin	1/22/2019	50	$75.00	$3,000.00	FALSE
b2437111	John	Bolt	341112434	Sales	7/24/2019	50	$44.30	$1,772.00	
a2437112	James	Phrase	670022435	Sales	2/24/2018	52	$19.90	$835.00	
b2437113	Luther	Miles	882012539	Marketing	6/3/2017	58	$15.00	$1,770.00	
2437114	Harry	Cliton	553112632	Sales	12/28/2019	58	$55.50	$1,623.00	
2437115	Bells	Simpson	125512442	Personnel	1/5/2017	45	$12.00	$430.00	
b2437116	Bob	Kelly	522001248	Human Resource	8/23/2019	45	$12.00	$430.00	
b2437117	Martins	April	538012498	Sales	8/13/2018	58	$15.50	$1,807.00	
2437118	James	Kingsley	587012489	Admin	9/27/2018	58	$49.00	$1,960.00	
2437119	Robert	Hume	480026440	Sales	10/7/2019	30	$55.95	$1,808.00	
b2437120	Harold	Jason	552812450	Sales	8/30/2019	30	$45.20	$1,920	
b2437121	David	Kessington	421596508	Sales	2/11/2019	25	$33.16	$1,025.85	
b2437122	Davis	Gray	207843531	Marketing	3/27/2017	30	$32.64	$1,012.66	
a2437123	Benjamin	Samuel	317960683	Marketing	5/7/2018	25	$32.12	$999.47	
b2437124	Anderson	Smith	527728054	Sales	2/21/2018	45	$31.59	$986.28	
a2437125	Wright	Clark	200968363	Director	7/17/2017	29	$31.07	$973.09	

This is simply because Mark Spencer works in the Admin department and not the sales department even though he has worked for 50 hours. So Mark Spencer failed to meet one of the conditions.

Now we can check for the other employees to see those who meet both conditions by click on the result for Mark Spencer, then hover the cursor on the fill handle and double-clicking as soon as the cursor turns to a black cross. Note that employees who fulfill only one of the conditions will be returned "False'" because the AND Function requires both conditions to be fulfilled to return "True."

Employee No	First Name	Last Name	SSN	Department	Employment Date	Hour	Rate	Gross	AND
					Midas Concept LLC				
					Payroll				
b2437110	Mark	Spencer	450012432	Admin	1/22/2019	50	$75.00	$3,000.00	FALSE
b2437111	John	Bolt	341112434	Sales	7/24/2019	50	$44.30	$1,772.00	TRUE
a2437112	James	Phrase	670022435	Sales	2/24/2018	52	$19.90	$835.00	FALSE
b2437113	Luther	Miles	882012539	Marketing	6/3/2017	58	$15.00	$1,770.00	FALSE
2437114	Harry	Cliton	553112632	Sales	12/28/2019	58	$55.50	$1,623.00	FALSE
2437115	Bells	Simpson	125512442	Personnel	1/5/2017	45	$12.00	$430.00	FALSE
b2437116	Bob	Kelly	522001248	Human Resource	8/23/2019	45	$12.00	$430.00	FALSE
b2437117	Martins	April	538012498	Sales	8/13/2018	58	$15.50	$1,807.00	FALSE
2437118	James	Kingsley	587012489	Admin	9/27/2018	58	$49.00	$1,960.00	FALSE
2437119	Robert	Hume	480026440	Sales	10/7/2019	30	$55.95	$1,808.00	FALSE
b2437120	Harold	Jason	552812450	Sales	8/30/2019	30	$45.20	$1,920	FALSE
b2437121	David	Kessington	421596508	Sales	2/11/2019	25	$33.16	$1,025.85	FALSE
b2437122	Davis	Gray	207843531	Marketing	3/27/2017	30	$32.64	$1,012.66	FALSE
a2437123	Benjamin	Samuel	317960683	Marketing	5/7/2018	25	$32.12	$999.47	FALSE
b2437124	Anderson	Smith	527728054	Sales	2/21/2018	45	$31.59	$986.28	FALSE
a2437125	Wright	Clark	200968363	Director	7/17/2017	29	$31.07	$973.09	FALSE

In our illustration, only one employee returned "True," and that employee is John Bolt. He is the only employee working in the Sales department and has worked for 50 hours.

The IF and the AND functions can be used together for logical calculations. For instance, if we have a list of pupils in a class that wrote both Mathematics and English Language test, and we want only those who passed both subjects, should be promoted to the next class. For this illustration, we will put our pass mark at 35 and above in each subject.

Pupils	Maths Score	English Score	Pass/Fail
A	30	53	
B	40	48	
C	25	65	
D	75	26	
E	52	33	
F	35	46	
G	66	41	
H	58	78	
I	70	66	

We can now write the formula to check if the first pupil should be promoted to the next class thus;

$$=IF(AND(C2>=35,D3>=35),\text{"Pass"},\text{"Fail"})$$

	B	C	D	E
SUM			f_x =IF(AND(C2>=35,D2>=35),"Pass","Fail")	
1	Pupils	Maths Score	English Score	Pass/Fail
2	A	30	53	=IF(AND(C2>=35,D2>=35),"Pass","Fail")
3	B	40	48	
4	C	25	65	
5	D	75	26	
6	E	52	33	
7	F	35	46	
8	G	66	41	
9	H	58	78	
10	I	70	66	

When you close the bracket and hit the ENTER key on the keyboard, it returns "Fail" for Pupil A. This is simply because He or she passed the English language test but Failed the Mathematics test. For this logical function to be "Pass," the Pupil must pass both subjects.

Now, let's find out how many of the students meet this condition by simply double-clicking on the fill handle with the black cross.

	B	C	D	E
E2			f_x =IF(AND(C2>=35,D2>=35),"Pass","Fail")	
1	Pupils	Maths Score	English Score	Pass/Fail
2	A	30	53	Fail
3	B	40	48	Pass
4	C	25	65	Fail
5	D	75	26	Fail
6	E	52	33	Fail
7	F	35	46	Pass
8	G	66	41	Pass
9	H	58	78	Pass
10	I	70	66	Pass

OR Function

The **OR Function** in Excel checks if one of the logical arguments of a function is valid and returns "True" and "False" if both arguments are not valid.

Unlike the AND Function, the OR Function will return a "True" result if one of the conditions is valid.

The general Syntax for the OR Function is;

$$=OR(Logic1, Logic2, Logic2, ...)$$

Let's illustrate with our Midas Concept LLC Payroll. This time around, let's look for employees who are either in the 'Sales' department or have worked for 50 Hours. Now, Excel will return True result if an employee fulfills any of these conditions for the OR function.

To get the OR Function for the first employee Mark Spencer, we use the function;

$$=OR(E29="Sales", G29=50)$$

	SUM		✗ ✓ fx	=OR(E29="Sales",G29=50)						
	A	B		D	E	F	G	H	I	J	K
25										
26						Midas Concept LLC				
27						Payroll				
28	Employee No	First Name	Last Name	SSN	Department	Employment Date	Hour	Rate	Gross	OR
29	b2437110	Mark	Spencer	450012432	Admin	1/22/2019	50	$75.00	$3,000.00	=OR(E29="Sales",G29=50)
30	b2437111	John	Bolt	341112434	Sales	7/24/2019	50	$44.30	$1,772.00	
31	a2437112	James	Phrase	670022435	Sales	2/24/2018	52	$19.90	$835.00	
32	b2437113	Luther	Miles	882012539	Marketing	6/3/2017	58	$15.00	$1,770.00	
33	2437114	Harry	Cliton	553112632	Sales	12/28/2019	58	$55.50	$1,623.00	
34	2437115	Bells	Simpson	125512442	Personnel	1/5/2017	45	$12.00	$430.00	
35	b2437116	Bob	Kelly	522001248	Human Resource	8/23/2019	45	$12.00	$430.00	
36	b2437117	Martins	April	538012498	Sales	8/13/2018	58	$15.50	$1,807.00	
37	2437118	James	Kingsley	587012489	Admin	9/27/2018	58	$49.00	$1,960.00	
38	2437119	Robert	Hume	480026440	Sales	10/7/2019	30	$55.95	$1,808.00	
39	b2437120	Harold	Jason	552812450	Sales	8/30/2019	30	$45.20	$1,920	
40	b2437121	David	Kessington	421596508	Sales	2/11/2019	25	$33.16	$1,025.85	
41	b2437122	Davis	Gray	207843531	Marketing	3/27/2017	30	$32.64	$1,012.66	
42	a2437123	Benjamin	Samuel	317960683	Marketing	5/7/2018	25	$32.12	$999.47	
43	a2437124	Anderson	Smith	527728054	Sales	2/21/2018	45	$31.59	$986.28	
44	a2437125	Wright	Clark	200968363	Director	7/17/2017	29	$31.07	$973.09	

When we hit the ENTER key on the keyboard, it returns "True" result for Mark Spencer because he fulfilled one of the conditions. Although he is not in the sales department, he has worked for 50 hours.

					Midas Concept LLC				
					Payroll				
Employee No	First Name	Last Name	SSN	Department	Employment Date	Hour	Rate	Gross	OR
b2437110	Mark	Spencer	450012432	Admin	1/22/2019	50	$75.00	$3,000.00	TRUE
b2437111	John	Bolt	341112434	Sales	7/24/2019	50	$44.30	$1,772.00	
a2437112	James	Phrase	670022435	Sales	2/24/2018	52	$19.90	$835.00	
b2437113	Luther	Miles	882012539	Marketing	6/3/2017	58	$15.00	$1,770.00	
2437114	Harry	Cliton	553112632	Sales	12/28/2019	58	$55.50	$1,623.00	
2437115	Bells	Simpson	125512442	Personnel	1/5/2017	45	$12.00	$430.00	
b2437116	Bob	Kelly	522001248	Human Resource	8/23/2019	45	$12.00	$430.00	
b2437117	Martins	April	538012498	Sales	8/13/2018	58	$15.50	$1,807.00	
2437118	James	Kingsley	587012489	Admin	9/27/2018	58	$49.00	$1,960.00	
2437119	Robert	Hume	480026440	Sales	10/7/2019	30	$55.95	$1,808.00	
b2437120	Harold	Jason	552812450	Sales	8/30/2019	30	$45.20	$1,920	
b2437121	David	Kessington	421596508	Sales	2/11/2019	25	$33.16	$1,025.85	
b2437122	Davis	Gray	207843531	Marketing	3/27/2017	30	$32.64	$1,012.66	
a2437123	Benjamin	Samuel	317960683	Marketing	5/7/2018	25	$32.12	$999.47	
b2437124	Anderson	Smith	527728054	Sales	2/21/2018	45	$31.59	$986.28	
a2437125	Wright	Clark	200968363	Director	7/17/2017	29	$31.07	$973.09	

Now, double-click on the fill handle to get the result for the other employees.

					Midas Concept LLC				
					Payroll				
Employee No	First Name	Last Name	SSN	Department	Employment Date	Hour	Rate	Gross	OR
b2437110	Mark	Spencer	450012432	Admin	1/22/2019	50	$75.00	$3,000.00	TRUE
b2437111	John	Bolt	341112434	Sales	7/24/2019	50	$44.30	$1,772.00	TRUE
a2437112	James	Phrase	670022435	Sales	2/24/2018	52	$19.90	$835.00	TRUE
b2437113	Luther	Miles	882012539	Marketing	6/3/2017	58	$15.00	$1,770.00	FALSE
2437114	Harry	Cliton	553112632	Sales	12/28/2019	58	$55.50	$1,623.00	TRUE
2437115	Bells	Simpson	125512442	Personnel	1/5/2017	45	$12.00	$430.00	FALSE
b2437116	Bob	Kelly	522001248	Human Resource	8/23/2019	45	$12.00	$430.00	FALSE
b2437117	Martins	April	538012498	Sales	8/13/2018	58	$15.50	$1,807.00	TRUE
2437118	James	Kingsley	587012489	Admin	9/27/2018	58	$49.00	$1,960.00	FALSE
2437119	Robert	Hume	480026440	Sales	10/7/2019	30	$55.95	$1,808.00	TRUE
b2437120	Harold	Jason	552812450	Sales	8/30/2019	30	$45.20	$1,920	TRUE
b2437121	David	Kessington	421596508	Sales	2/11/2019	25	$33.16	$1,025.85	TRUE
b2437122	Davis	Gray	207843531	Marketing	3/27/2017	30	$32.64	$1,012.66	FALSE
a2437123	Benjamin	Samuel	317960683	Marketing	5/7/2018	25	$32.12	$999.47	FALSE
b2437124	Anderson	Smith	527728054	Sales	2/21/2018	45	$31.59	$986.28	TRUE
a2437125	Wright	Clark	200968363	Director	7/17/2017	29	$31.07	$973.09	FALSE

Exercise: Use the **AND Function** to identify Employees in the Marketing Department who have also worked for 30 hours.

Exercise 2: Use the OR Function to identify Employees in the Marketing Department or have worked for 45 hours.

We can also use the IF Function and the OR Function together. Let's take, for example, pupils in a class wrote a Mathematics and English Language test, and they are required to pass at least one of the subjects to be promoted to the next class. The pass mark is 35 and above.

	Pupils	Maths Score	English Score	Promoted/Not Promoted
1	Pupils	Maths Score	English Score	Promoted/Not Promoted
2	A	30	53	
3	B	40	48	
4	C	25	65	
5	D	75	26	
6	E	52	33	
7	F	35	46	
8	G	66	41	
9	H	58	78	
10	I	70	66	

Here we can use the IF and OR Function to execute this task.

=IF(OR(C2>=35,D2>=35),"Promoted", "Not Promoted")

	Pupils	Maths Score	English Score	Promoted/Not Promoted
1	Pupils	Maths Score	English Score	Promoted/Not Promoted
2	A	30	53	=IF(OR(C2>=35,D2>=35),"Promoted","Not Promoted")
3	B	40	48	
4	C	25	65	
5	D	75	26	
6	E	52	33	
7	F	35	46	
8	G	66	41	
9	H	58	78	
10	I	70	66	

When we close the bracket and hit the ENTER key on the keyboard, the Function returns "Promoted" for the first pupil because he fulfilled one of the conditions.

He Passed the English language test even though he failed the Mathematics test.

	B	C	D	E
	C13		f_x	
1	Pupils	Maths Score	English Score	Promoted/Not Promoted
2	A	30	53	Promoted
3	B	40	48	
4	C	25	65	
5	D	75	26	
6	E	52	33	
7	F	35	46	
8	G	66	41	
9	H	58	78	
10	I	70	66	

Now, double-click on the fill handle with the black cross to get the list of those promoted and those who were not.

	B	C	D	E
	E2		f_x =IF(OR(C2>=35,D2>=35),"Promoted","Not Promoted")	
1	Pupils	Maths Score	English Score	Promoted/Not Promoted
2	A	30	53	Promoted
3	B	40	48	Promoted
4	C	25	65	Promoted
5	D	75	26	Promoted
6	E	52	33	Promoted
7	F	35	46	Promoted
8	G	66	41	Promoted
9	H	58	78	Promoted
10	I	70	66	Promoted

In our illustration, they were all promoted because they fulfilled the condition required for promotion to the next class.

NOT Function

The **NOT Function** returns the opposite of a given value. Let's look at the **NOT Function** using the example on our worksheet.

The Syntax for **NOT Function** is;

$$=NOT(logical)$$

	A	B	C
1	Pupils	Maths Score	NOT
2	A	30	
3	B	40	
4	C	25	
5	D	75	
6	E	52	
7	F	35	
8	G	66	
9	H	58	
10	I	70	

In our illustration, we want to use the **NOT Function** to identify Pupils who failed the mathematics test. The pass mark is 35 and anything less than 35 is regarded as fail, and any score above 35 is Pass. So we check for pupil A.

$$=NOT(B1>35)$$

If the score is less than 35, then it returns a FALSE statement. Which means the pupil failed the test.

SUM		✕ ✓ f_x	=NOT(B1>35)	
	A	B	C	D
1	Pupils	Maths Score	NOT	
2	A	30	=NOT(B1>35)	
3	B	40		
4	C	25		
5	D	75		
6	E	52		
7	F	35		
8	G	66		
9	H	58		
10	I	70		

When we hit the ENTER key on the keyboard, it returns a FALSE statement because the score of Pupil A is below 35; hence he failed the test.

	A	B	C
1	Pupils	Maths Score	NOT
2	A	30	FALSE
3	B	40	
4	C	25	
5	D	75	
6	E	52	
7	F	35	
8	G	66	
9	H	58	
10	I	70	

Now, copy the function into the remaining cells to ascertain those who failed and those who passed the examination using the NOT Function.

	A	B	C
1	Pupils	Maths Score	NOT
2	A	30	FALSE
3	B	40	TRUE
4	C	25	FALSE
5	D	75	TRUE
6	E	52	FALSE
7	F	35	FALSE
8	G	66	TRUE
9	H	58	FALSE
10	I	70	FALSE

The **NOT Function** is also used in combination with the **IF Function**. For instance, we can say

$$=IF(NOT(B2>35)$$

This means Pupils, who do not score more than 35 is said to have FAILED, so we used "Fail" in place of "True" and the Pass in place of "False." So we can re-write our function thus;

$$=IF(NOT(B2>35),"Fail","Pass")$$

	SUM	▾ ⊙ ✗ ✔ fx	=IF(NOT(B2>35),"Fail","Pass")		
	A	B	C	D	E
1	Pupils	Maths Score	NOT		
2	A	=IF(NOT(B2>35),"Fail","Pass")			
3	B	40			
4	C	25			
5	D	75			
6	E	52			
7	F	35			
8	G	66			
9	H	58			
10	I	70			

So, in this case, Pupil A Failed the test. Now, we can copy the function into other cells to see if they failed the test or Passed.

	C2	▾ ⊙	fx	=IF(NOT(B2>35),"Fail","Pass")	
	A	B	C	D	E
1	Pupils	Maths Score	NOT		
2	A	30	Fail		
3	B	40	Pass		
4	C	25	Fail		
5	D	75	Pass		
6	E	52	Pass		
7	F	35	Fail		
8	G	66	Pass		
9	H	58	Pass		
10	I	70	Pass		

XOR Function

The XOR function checks if one and only one condition is valid. If there are two conditions, the XOR function returns 'True' if one condition is 'valid.' If none of the conditions are valid, then it returns 'False.' Let's see how we can use the XOR Function; let's say we want to purchase a new smartphone, and we have two specifications of the phone we need to consider before buying it. They are – the storage and the RAM size.

	G11	▾	f_x	
	A	B	C	D
1	Smart Phone	Storage	RAM	XOR
2	1	512	5	
3	2	1000	6	
4	3	512	7	
5	4	1000	8	
6	5	400	6	
7	6	200	17	
8	7	512	5	
9	8	128	7	
10	9	512	4	
11	10	1000	9	

We want to select a phone with at least 500GB of storage, and a RAM greater than 8GB. So the two conditions are

$$Storage \geq 500GB$$

$$RAM > 8GB$$

Now, we check the first cell to see if our conditions for buying the smartphone is valid.

$$=XOR(B2>=500,C2>8)$$

88

	SUM	▾	× ✓ fx	=XOR(B2>=500,C2>8)	

	A	B	C	D	E
1	Smart Phone	Storage	RAM	XOR	
2	1	512		=XOR(B2>=500,C2>8)	
3	2	1000	6		
4	3	512	7		
5	4	1000	8		
6	5	400	6		
7	6	200	17		
8	7	512	5		
9	8	128	7		
10	9	512	4		
11	10	1000	9		

If the function returns a 'True' statement, it means the phone met the XOR condition.

	A	B	C	D
1	Smart Phone	Storage	RAM	XOR
2	1	512	5	TRUE
3	2	1000	6	TRUE
4	3	512	7	TRUE
5	4	1000	8	TRUE
6	5	400	6	FALSE
7	6	200	17	TRUE
8	7	512	5	TRUE
9	8	128	7	FALSE
10	9	512	4	TRUE
11	10	1000	9	TRUE

The smartphones that return 'True' are the ones we can buy because one of the conditions is fulfilled.

The XOR Function can be used in combination with the IF Function. When the XOR and IF Function is combined, it checks if the condition is met and returns one value if 'True' and another value if 'False.'

IFERROR Function

When working with Excel, we sometimes encounter errors, and these errors can be harsh only, harsh+value, harsh+reference, DIV, etc. The **IFERROR Function** is used to identify these errors in Excel.

The general syntax is;

=IFERROR(Cell address, "Output")

The **IFERROR Function** is used to replace error messages in cells with zeroes (0). What this means is that you can use zero (0) to replace whatever error type in a cell. This is done to give our worksheet a cleaner look. If, for instance, we have a Cell C2 with a DIV error, we can replace that cell with a zero (0) using the **IFERROR function**. This is written thus;

=IFERROR(C2,0)

Close the bracket and hit the ENTER key on the Keyboard. Drag the formula across the column and every other cell with a DIV error is replaced with a zero (0).

IFNA Function

IFNA function returns the value user specifies in the expression whenever the function encounters the #N/A error; otherwise, the function returns the cell value.

The general syntax for IFNA Function is;

=IFNA(Cell Address, "Output")

#N/A errors are referencing errors. They come up when we are not giving the right cell reference in a formula. To ensure we don't hide the reference errors, we use the IFNA Function. In our illustration below, we have a row (J:J) with a list of errors (#N/A, BBI, and BMS errors) and we want to replace all the #N/A errors in column J with "No Data Available" to make our worksheet look neat. Starting with the first cell (J29), we type

=IFNA(J29,"No Data Available")

First Name	Last Name	SSN	Department	Employment Date	Hour	Rate	Gross	N/A Errors	
				Midas Concept LLC					
				Payroll					
First Name	**Last Name**	**SSN**	**Department**	**Employment Date**	**Hour**	**Rate**	**Gross**	**N/A Errors**	
Mark	Spencer	450012432	Admin	1/22/2019	50	$75.00	$3,000.00	#N/A	=IFNA(J29,"No Data Available")
John	Bolt	341112434	Sales	7/24/2019	50	$44.30	$1,772.00	#N/A	
James	Phrase	670022435	Sales	2/24/2018	52	$19.90	$835.00	#N/A	
Luther	Miles	882012539	Marketing	6/3/2017	58	$15.00	$1,770.00	#N/A	
Harry	Cliton	553112632	Sales	12/28/2019	58	$55.50	$1,623.00	BBI	
Bells	Simpson	125512442	Personnel	1/5/2017	45	$12.00	$430.00	BBI	
Bob	Kelly	522001248	Human Resource	8/23/2019	45	$12.00	$430.00	#N/A	
Martins	April	538012498	Sales	8/13/2018	58	$15.50	$1,807.00	#N/A	
James	Kingsley	587012489	Admin	9/27/2018	58	$49.00	$1,960.00	#N/A	
Robert	Hume	480026440	Sales	10/7/2019	30	$55.95	$1,808.00	BMS	
Harold	Jason	552812450	Sales	8/30/2019	30	$45.20	$1,920	BMS	
David	Kessington	421596508	Sales	2/11/2019	25	$33.16	$1,025.85	#N/A	
Davis	Gray	207843531	Marketing	3/27/2017	30	$32.64	$1,012.66	BMS	
Benjamin	Samuel	317960683	Marketing	5/7/2018	25	$32.12	$999.47	#N/A	
Anderson	Smith	527728054	Sales	2/21/2018	45	$31.59	$986.28	#N/A	
Wright	Clark	200968363	Director	7/17/2017	29	$31.07	$973.09		

Now, we can drag the function across the column to identify cells with #N/A errors.

	Last Name	SSN	Department	Employment Date	Hour	Rate	Gross	N/A Errors	
				Midas Concept LLC					
				Payroll					
	Last Name	**SSN**	**Department**	**Employment Date**	**Hour**	**Rate**	**Gross**	**N/A Errors**	
	Spencer	450012432	Admin	1/22/2019	50	$75.00	$3,000.00	#N/A	No Data Available
	Bolt	341112434	Sales	7/24/2019	50	$44.30	$1,772.00	#N/A	No Data Available
	Phrase	670022435	Sales	2/24/2018	52	$19.90	$835.00	#N/A	No Data Available
	Miles	882012539	Marketing	6/3/2017	58	$15.00	$1,770.00	#N/A	No Data Available
	Cliton	553112632	Sales	12/28/2019	58	$55.50	$1,623.00	BBI	BBI
	Simpson	125512442	Personnel	1/5/2017	45	$12.00	$430.00	BBI	BBI
	Kelly	522001248	Human Resource	8/23/2019	45	$12.00	$430.00	#N/A	No Data Available
	April	538012498	Sales	8/13/2018	58	$15.50	$1,807.00	#N/A	No Data Available
	Kingsley	587012489	Admin	9/27/2018	58	$49.00	$1,960.00	#N/A	No Data Available
	Hume	480026440	Sales	10/7/2019	30	$55.95	$1,808.00	BMS	BMS
	Jason	552812450	Sales	8/30/2019	30	$45.20	$1,920	BMS	BMS
	Kessington	421596508	Sales	2/11/2019	25	$33.16	$1,025.85	#N/A	No Data Available
	Gray	207843531	Marketing	3/27/2017	30	$32.64	$1,012.66	BMS	BMS
	Samuel	317960683	Marketing	5/7/2018	25	$32.12	$999.47	#N/A	No Data Available
	Smith	527728054	Sales	2/21/2018	45	$31.59	$986.28	#N/A	No Data Available

Error Checking

Error checking helps users to identify the cells where an error has occurred. To use error checking,

- Click on the 'Formulas' tab
- Click on Error Checking button

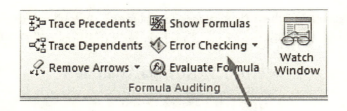

A window will pop up, indicating which cells with an error. This is very useful when you have a big list of data, and you have entered formulas in different parts of the sheet.

NESTED IF Function

NESTED IF Function checks the logics specified by users in the multi-layered IF functions and returns the output for the **IF Function**, which is correct. There is no limit on the number of IF Functions within a **NESTED IF Function**; users can apply as many **IF Functions** he or she wants.

The general syntax for the **NESTED IF Function** is;

**=IF(Logic1,"Output1", IF(Logic2,"Output2",
IF(Logic3,"Output3","Value if false").**

Let's look at an illustration using the Midas Concept LLC payroll worksheet.

Employee No	First Name	Last Name	SSN	Department	Employment Date	Hour	Rate	Gross	Bonus
				Midas Concept LLC					
				Payroll					
b2437110	Mark	Spencer	450012432	Admin	1/22/2019	50	$75.00	$3,000.00	
b2437111	John	Bolt	341112434	Sales	7/24/2019	50	$44.30	$1,772.00	
a2437112	James	Phrase	670022435	Sales	2/24/2018	52	$19.90	$835.00	
b2437113	Luther	Miles	882012539	Marketing	6/3/2017	58	$15.00	$1,770.00	
2437114	Harry	Cliton	553112632	Sales	12/28/2019	58	$55.50	$1,623.00	
2437115	Bells	Simpson	125512442	Personnel	1/5/2017	45	$12.00	$430.00	
b2437116	Bob	Kelly	522001248	Human Resource	8/23/2019	45	$12.00	$430.00	
b2437117	Martins	April	538012498	Sales	8/13/2018	58	$15.50	$1,807.00	
2437118	James	Kingsley	587012489	Admin	9/27/2018	58	$49.00	$1,960.00	
2437119	Robert	Hume	480026440	Sales	10/7/2019	30	$55.95	$1,808.00	
b2437120	Harold	Jason	552812450	Sales	8/30/2019	30	$45.20	$1,920	
b2437121	David	Kessington	421596508	Sales	2/11/2019	25	$33.16	$1,025.85	
b2437122	Davis	Gray	207843531	Marketing	3/27/2017	30	$32.64	$1,012.66	
a2437123	Benjamin	Samuel	317960683	Marketing	5/7/2018	25	$32.12	$999.47	
b2437124	Anderson	Smith	527728054	Sales	2/21/2018	45	$31.59	$986.28	
a2437125	Wright	Clark	200968363	Director	7/17/2017	29	$31.07	$973.09	

92

Let's assume Management has decided to give out some amount as a bonus based on the employee's department using the table below.

Department	Bonus Amount
Sales	$1000
Marketing	$500
Human Resource	$200
Others	$100

So, Management is giving a total of $1000 to employees in the sales department, $500 to those in the Marketing department, $200 to those in Human Resources and those in other departments would take $100 each as a bonus. We can use the NESTED IF function to implement this on our worksheet. We start by checking if Mark Spencer is in the sales department. If yes, give him $1000, else check If he is in Marketing department, if true, give him $500, else check if he is in Human Resource department, if true, give him $200 but if none of the conditions is fulfilled give him $100.

=IF(E29="Sales",1000,IF(E29="Marketing",500,IF(E29="Human Resource",200,100)))

	SUM			=IF(E29="Sales",1000,IF(E29="Marketing",500,IF(E29="Human Resource",200,100))						
	A	B	C	D	E	F	G	H	I	
25										
26					**Midas Concept LLC**					
27					Payroll					
28	Employee No	First Name	Last Name	SSN	Department	Employment Date	Hour	Rate	Gross	Bonus
29	b2437110	Mark	Spencer	450012432	Admin	1/22/2019	50	$75.00	$3,000.00	=IF(E29="Sales",1000,IF(E29="Marketing",
30	b2437111	John	Bolt	341112434	Sales	7/24/2019	50	$44.30	$1,772.00	500,IF(E29="Human Resource",200,100)))
31	a2437112	James	Phrase	670022435	Sales	2/24/2018	52	$19.90	$835.00	[logical_test, [value_if_true], [value_if_false]]
32	b2437113	Luther	Miles	882012539	Marketing	6/3/2017	58	$15.00	$1,770.00	
33	2437114	Harry	Cliton	553112632	Sales	12/28/2019	58	$55.50	$1,623.00	
34	2437115	Bells	Simpson	125512442	Personnel	1/5/2017	45	$12.00	$430.00	
35	b2437116	Bob	Kelly	522001248	Human Resource	8/23/2019	45	$12.00	$430.00	
36	b2437117	Martins	April	538012498	Sales	8/13/2018	58	$15.50	$1,807.00	
37	2437118	James	Kingsley	587012489	Admin	9/27/2018	58	$49.00	$1,960.00	
38	2437119	Robert	Hume	480026440	Sales	10/7/2019	30	$55.95	$1,808.00	
39	b2437120	Harold	Jason	552812450	Sales	8/30/2019	30	$45.20	$1,920	
40	b2437121	David	Kessington	421596508	Sales	2/11/2019	25	$33.16	$1,025.85	
41	b2437122	Davis	Gray	207843531	Marketing	3/27/2017	30	$32.64	$1,012.66	
42	a2437123	Benjamin	Samuel	317960683	Marketing	5/7/2018	25	$32.12	$999.47	
43	b2437124	Anderson	Smith	527728054	Sales	2/21/2018	45	$31.59	$986.28	
44	a2437125	Wright	Clark	200968363	Director	7/17/2017	29	$31.07	$973.09	

When we press the ENTER key on the keyboard, we get the result for the first employee. Now, we can duplicate the formula for all the employees and see those who satisfy the conditions and the bonus they got.

Midas Concept LLC

Payroll

Employee No	First Name	Last Name	SSN	Department	Employment Date	Hour	Rate	Gross	Bonus
b2437110	Mark	Spencer	450012432	Admin	1/22/2019	50	$75.00	$3,000.00	100
b2437111	John	Bolt	341112434	Sales	7/24/2019	50	$44.30	$1,772.00	
a2437112	James	Phrase	670022435	Sales	2/24/2018	52	$19.90	$835.00	
b2437113	Luther	Miles	882012539	Marketing	6/3/2017	58	$15.00	$1,770.00	
2437114	Harry	Cliton	553112632	Sales	12/28/2019	58	$55.50	$1,623.00	
2437115	Bells	Simpson	125512442	Personnel	1/5/2017	45	$12.00	$430.00	
b2437116	Bob	Kelly	522001248	Human Resource	8/23/2019	45	$12.00	$430.00	
b2437117	Martins	April	538012498	Sales	8/13/2018	58	$15.50	$1,807.00	
2437118	James	Kingsley	587012489	Admin	9/27/2018	58	$49.00	$1,960.00	
2437119	Robert	Hume	480026440	Sales	10/7/2019	30	$55.95	$1,808.00	
b2437120	Harold	Jason	552812450	Sales	8/30/2019	30	$45.20	$1,920	
b2437121	David	Kessington	421596508	Sales	2/11/2019	25	$33.16	$1,025.85	
b2437122	Davis	Gray	207843531	Marketing	3/27/2017	30	$32.64	$1,012.66	
a2437123	Benjamin	Samuel	317960683	Marketing	5/7/2018	25	$32.12	$999.47	
b2437124	Anderson	Smith	527728054	Sales	2/21/2018	45	$31.59	$986.28	
a2437125	Wright	Clark	200968363	Director	7/17/2017	29	$31.07	$973.09	

The first employee got $100 because he is not in Sales, nor Marketing nor Human Resource Department, hence he belongs to others. Now, let's duplicate the formula across all employees to find out how much bonus they are to get.

Midas Concept LLC

Payroll

Employee No	First Name	Last Name	SSN	Department	Employment Date	Hour	Rate	Gross	Bonus
b2437110	Mark	Spencer	450012432	Admin	1/22/2019	50	$75.00	$3,000.00	100
b2437111	John	Bolt	341112434	Sales	7/24/2019	50	$44.30	$1,772.00	1000
a2437112	James	Phrase	670022435	Sales	2/24/2018	52	$19.90	$835.00	1000
b2437113	Luther	Miles	882012539	Marketing	6/3/2017	58	$15.00	$1,770.00	500
2437114	Harry	Cliton	553112632	Sales	12/28/2019	58	$55.50	$1,623.00	1000
2437115	Bells	Simpson	125512442	Personnel	1/5/2017	45	$12.00	$430.00	100
b2437116	Bob	Kelly	522001248	Human Resource	8/23/2019	45	$12.00	$430.00	200
b2437117	Martins	April	538012498	Sales	8/13/2018	58	$15.50	$1,807.00	1000
2437118	James	Kingsley	587012489	Admin	9/27/2018	58	$49.00	$1,960.00	100
2437119	Robert	Hume	480026440	Sales	10/7/2019	30	$55.95	$1,808.00	1000
b2437120	Harold	Jason	552812450	Sales	8/30/2019	30	$45.20	$1,920	1000
b2437121	David	Kessington	421596508	Sales	2/11/2019	25	$33.16	$1,025.85	1000
b2437122	Davis	Gray	207843531	Marketing	3/27/2017	30	$32.64	$1,012.66	500
a2437123	Benjamin	Samuel	317960683	Marketing	5/7/2018	25	$32.12	$999.47	500
b2437124	Anderson	Smith	527728054	Sales	2/21/2018	45	$31.59	$986.28	1000
a2437125	Wright	Clark	200968363	Director	7/17/2017	29	$31.07	$973.09	100

Chapter Five

Text Functions

There are several TEXT Functions in Excel - LOWER Function, UPPER Function, Proper Function, Left Function, Right Function, MID Function,

LOWER Function

The LOWER Function converts the cell value to lower case letters. In other words, it converts all the text in a cell to a lower case.

The general syntax for **LOWER Function** is

$$=LOWER(Cell address)$$

e.g.

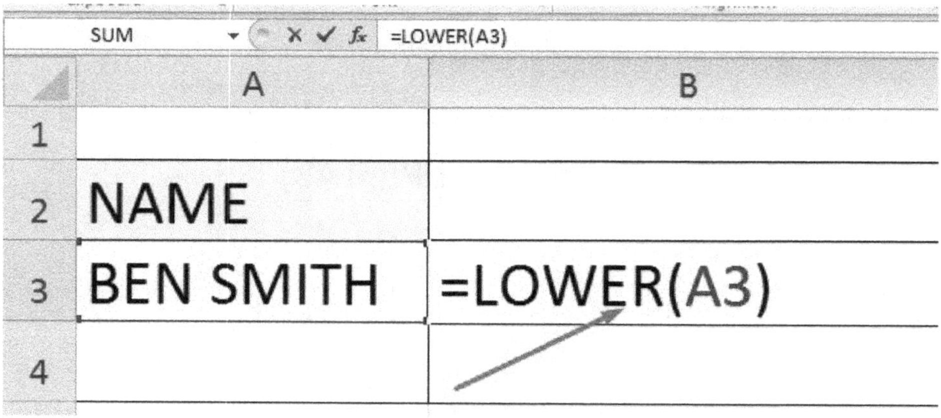

	A	B
	SUM ▾ × ✓ fx =LOWER(A3)	
1		
2	NAME	
3	BEN SMITH	=LOWER(A3)
4		

When we hit the ENTER key on the keyboard we get.

	A	B
1		
2	NAME	
3	BEN SMITH	ben smith
4		

UPPER Function

UPPER Function converts the cell value to upper case letters. In other words, it converts all the text in a cell to an upper case.

The general syntax for **UPPER Function** is

$$=UPPER(Cell\ address)$$

e.g.

	A	B
1		
2	NAME	
3	Chris Charles	=UPPER(A3)
4		

When you hit the ENTER key on the keyboard, you get

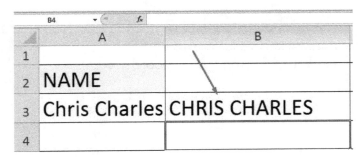

	A	B
1		
2	NAME	
3	Chris Charles	CHRIS CHARLES
4		

PROPER Function

PROPER Function converts the first later into upper case while changing the rest of the text to lower case.

	A	B
	SUM ▾ (× ✓ ƒx =PROPER(A3)	
1		
2	NAME	
3	JASON FREEMAN	=PROPER(A3)
4		

When we hit the ENTER key, we get the proper function result for Jason Freeman.

	A	B
	B4 ▾ (ƒx	
1		
2	NAME	
3	JASON FREEMAN	Jason Freeman
4		

LEFT Function

LEFT Function extracts a given number of characters from the left side of the supplied text or string.

The General syntax is

$$=LEFT(Text,[num\_chars])$$

Where 'Text' is the text we want to extract a LEFT Function from and 'num_chars' is the number of characters to be extracted from the text.

Let's use the sheet below for our illustration.

	A	B	C
1			
2	FIRST NAME	LAST NAME	Left Function
3	Jason	Freeman	
4			

We have the column for First Name and another column for the Last Name. We can perform a LEFT Function on Jason, which is in cell A3 and specify the number of characters to be extracted from the left of Jason. We type;

=LEFT(A3,3)

	A	B	C
1			
2	FIRST NAME	LAST NAME	Left Function
3	Jason	Freeman	=LEFT(A3,3)
4			

Where A3 is the cell holding the text, Jason and 3 is the number of characters to be extracted from Jason.

When we hit the ENTER key on the keyboard, we have

C4	▼	fx	
	A	B	C
1			
2	FIRST NAME	LAST NAME	Left Function
3	Jason	Freeman	Jas
4			

We have extracted the first three characters from the left side of 'Jason', which is 'Jas.' Let's increase the number of characters [num_char] to 4.

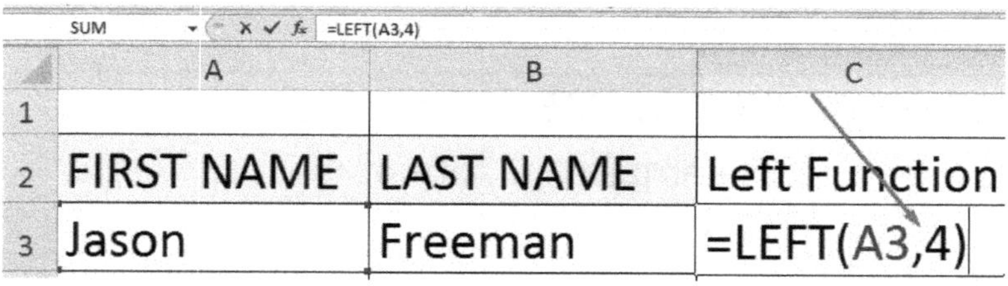

	A	B	C
	SUM ▾ X ✓ ƒx =LEFT(A3,4)		
1			
2	FIRST NAME	LAST NAME	Left Function
3	Jason	Freeman	=LEFT(A3,4)

Here is what we got when we hit the ENTER key

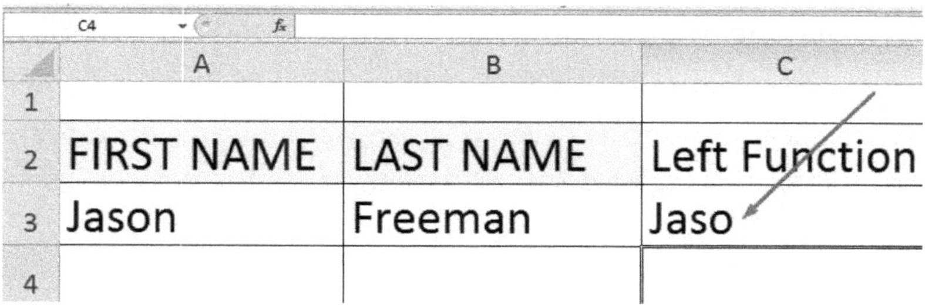

	A	B	C
	C4 ▾ ƒx		
1			
2	FIRST NAME	LAST NAME	Left Function
3	Jason	Freeman	Jaso
4			

RIGHT Function

RIGHT function extracts a given number of characters from the right side of the supplied text or string.

The General syntax is

=RIGHT(Text,[num_chars})

For instance, let's do the right function for the text in Cell B3, using four(4) characters.

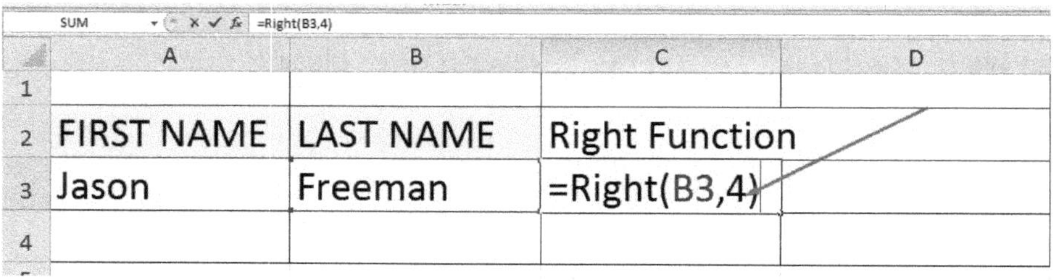

	A	B	C	D
	SUM ▾ X ✓ ƒx =Right(B3,4)			
1				
2	FIRST NAME	LAST NAME	Right Function	
3	Jason	Freeman	=Right(B3,4)	
4				

Hit the ENTER key on the keyboard

	A	B	C	D
1				
2	FIRST NAME	LAST NAME	Right Function	
3	Jason	Freeman	eman	
4				

MID Function

The **MID Function** works similarly to the LEFT and the RIGHT. It does not extract characters from the left or the right, but the middle of the text where you are required to provide a given position and a certain amount of characters from the start point. The general syntax is given as

$$=MID(Text,[num\_char],[num\_char))$$

	A	B	C
1			
2	FIRST NAME	LAST NAME	MID Function
3	Jason	Freeman	=MID(B3,3,3)
			MID(text, start_num, num_chars)
4			
5			
6			
7			
8			

When we hit the ENTER key on the keyboard after closing the bracket we have

⊿	A	B	C
1			
2	FIRST NAME	LAST NAME	MID Function
3	Jason	Freeman	eem
4			

LEN Function

The **Len Function** returns the number of characters in a string. The LEN is short for **LENGTH**. So we use the **LEN Function** to ascertain the length of a cell. The general syntax for the **LEN Function** is

$$=LEN(Cell1)$$

Let's use the worksheet below to illustrate the LEN Function. For instance, if we want to know the number of characters in 'Oranges' in our spread-sheet, we use the **LEN Function**. 'Oranges' is in Cell B4).

⊿	A	B	C	D	E
1	Order ID	Product	Unit Price	Quantity	
2	23412	Eggs	$14.00	10	
3	23413	Carrots	$9.90	12	
4	23414	Oranges	$14.90	9	
5	23415	Mangoes	$17.60	5	
6	23416	Grapes	$40.20	30	
7	23417	Pears	$26.50	35	
8					

To do this, we say

$$=LEN(B4)$$

	A	B	C	D	E	F
	SUM		▾	× ✓ *fx* =LEN(B4)		
1	Order ID	Product	Unit Price	Quantity		
2	23412	Eggs	$14.00	10		LEN
3	23413	Carrots	$9.90	12		=LEN(B4)
4	23414	Oranges	$14.90	9		
5	23415	Mangoes	$17.60	5		
6	23416	Grapes	$40.20	30		
7	23417	Pears	$26.50	35		

We get the answer, 7. Oranges consist of seven (7) characters.

	A	B	C	D	E	F
1	Order ID	Product	Unit Price	Quantity		
2	23412	Eggs	$14.00	10		LEN
3	23413	Carrots	$9.90	12		7
4	23414	Oranges	$14.90	9		
5	23415	Mangoes	$17.60	5		
6	23416	Grapes	$40.20	30		
7	23417	Pears	$26.50	35		

Note: if there is a space before or after a character, the LEN Function will count it. Space is also a character.

EXACT Function

The **EXACT Function** returns True if the content of two selected cells are the same but returns false if the content of the two cells is not the same. Note that the **EXACT Function** is case sensitive. The general syntax for the **EXACT Function** is given thus;

$$=EXACT(text1,text2)$$

Let's now compare the contents of the sheet below

	A	B	C
1			
2			EXACT Function
3	Jason	Freeman	=EXACT(A3,B3)
4	Apple	APPLE	
5	Orange	Orange	
6	ORANEGE	Orange	
7	Apple	Apple	
8	apple	apple	

When we hit the ENTER key we get a True or False result.

	A	B	C
1			
2			EXACT Function
3	Jason	Freeman	FALSE
4	Apple	APPLE	
5	Orange	Orange	
6	ORANEGE	Orange	
7	Apple	Apple	
8	apple	apple	

Now let's compare the remaining items on the sheet to find out if they are exactly the same or not.

	C3	▾ (	fx =EXACT(A3,B3)	

◢	A	B	C
1			
2			EXACT Function
3	Jason	Freeman	FALSE
4	Apple	APPLE	FALSE
5	Orange	Orange	TRUE
6	ORANEGE	Orange	FALSE
7	Apple	Apple	TRUE
8	apple	apple	TRUE

RANDBETWEEN Function

The **RANDBETWEEN Function** returns a random number between selected values. The General syntax for **RANDBETWEEN Function** is written thus;

=RANDBETWEEN(cell address1, cell address2) or

=RANDBETWEEN(cell address, Value)

Note that value in cell address2 has to be higher than the value in cell address1.

For instance, we have 40 in a cell and 200 in a separate cell, and we use the RANDBETWEEN function, which will return random values between 40 and 200. Let's use the sheet below to carry it out.

	SUM	▾ (X ✓ fx =RANDBETWEEN(A1,B1)	

◢	A	B	C
1	40	200	=RANDBETWEEN(A1,B1)
2			

When we hit the ENTER Key, we get a result.

C1		f_x =RANDBETWEEN(A1,B1)	
	A	B	C
1	40	200	125
2			

125 is a number between 40 and 200. Any time you click on the "Calculate sheet" under the 'Formulas' tab and in the 'Calculation' group.

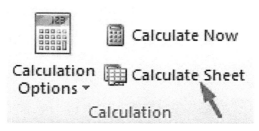

The result for the **RANDBETWEEN Function** changes to another value, which is stil between 40 and 200.

Chapter Six
More Excel Tips

AutoFIll Options

When using the Fill handle to copy the content of one cell to another, the AutoFill options sometimes pop up for you to select what type of reference should be copied into the new cell(s).

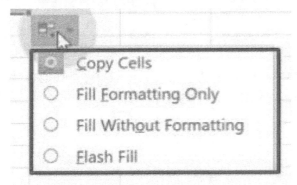

By default, the "Copy Cells" option copies exactly what is in the cell to the target cell. If you wish to copy the formatting of the cell to the target cell without copying its content, we use the "Fill Formatting Only" option. For instance, if the previous cell has a pre-set font size, color, or italics, bold, etc., you can apply these formats to a targeted cell without copying its content using the "Fill Formatting Only" option. The fill without formatting option copies the content of the previous cell into the new cell without applying the format of the cell you are copying from.

The Flash Fill is part of the AutoFill feature. To use this feature, you need to be next to a column of data you want to change or you could be several columns away as long as it is within the same database range. The Flash Fill looks at a pattern and automatically follows that pattern. Let's use the example below for our illustration. We have a database with Last Names, Middle Names and First Names as well as another column labeled Name (cell D1).

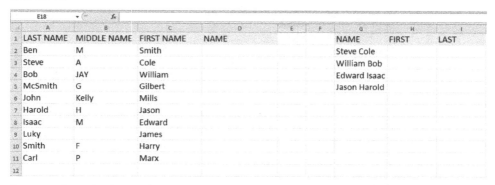

To use the Flash Fill feature, in the column labeled "Name," we begin by typing a couple of names to establish a pattern for Excel Flash Fill to follow. For instance, we type in the Last and First Name within the "Name" column separated by a comma. When we do this, excel sees a pattern and automatically gives us a list of names based on this pattern.

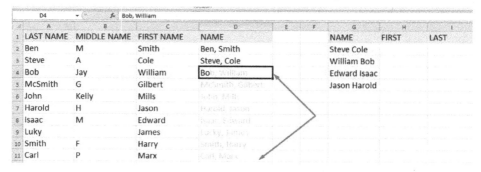

We have the option to accept this list or reject it. To accept the list, hit the ENTER key on the keyboard, and it fills it in a flash.

	A	B	C	D	E	F	G	H	I
1	LAST NAME	MIDDLE NAME	FIRST NAME	NAME			NAME	FIRST	LAST
2	Ben	M	Smith	Ben, Smith			Steve Cole		
3	Steve	A	Cole	Steve, Cole			William Bob		
4	Bob	Jay	William	Bob, William			Edward Isaac		
5	McSmith	G	Gilbert	McSmith, Gilbert			Jason Harold		
6	John	Kelly	Mills	John, Mills					
7	Harold	H	Jason	Harold, Jason					
8	Isaac	M	Edward	Isaac, Edward					
9	Luky		James	Lucky, James					
10	Smith	F	Harry	Smith, Harry					
11	Carl	P	Marx	Carl, Marx					

This brings up the flash fill option where you can "undo Flash fill", "Accept Suggestions," or "select all changed cells."

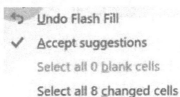

↩ Undo Flash Fill

✓ Accept suggestions

Select all 0 blank cells

Select all 8 changed cells

If the Flash Fill doesn't work for you, it may likely be turned off in the Excel Options. To turn it ON, click on "File" > "Options" > "Advanced" > turn ON "Automatically Flash Fill" option and click "OK."

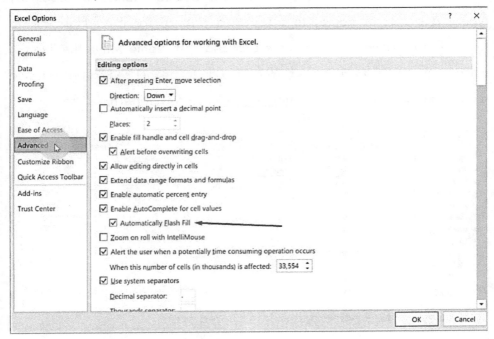

From our example, we could type in some names into the column for the First Name, and Flash Fill will automatically populate the other cells following our pattern. Click on Enter key on the keyboard to accept the Flash Fill suggestion.

MIDDLE NAME	FIRST NAME	NAME		NAME	FIRST	LAST
M	Smith	Ben, Smith		Steve Cole	Steve	
A	Cole	Steve, Cole		William Bob	William	
Jay	William	Bob, William		Edward Isaac	Edward	
G	Gilbert	McSmith, Gilbert		Jason Harold	Jason	
Kelly	Mills	John, Mills				
H	Jason	Harold, Jason				
M	Edward	Isaac, Edward				
	James	Lucky, James				
F	Harry	Smith, Harry				
P	Marx	Carl, Marx				

Alternatively, after typing the first two names, click on Ctrl+E to Flash Fill the remaining cells. Ctrl+E is the shortcut for the Flash Fill option. We can also Flash Fill the Last Name for our example above using the same approach.

	A	B	C	D	E	F	G	H	I	J	K
1	LAST NAME	MIDDLE NAME	FIRST NAME	NAME			NAME	FIRST	LAST		
2	Ben	M	Smith	Ben, Smith			Steve Cole	Steve	Cole		
3	Steve	A	Cole	Steve, Cole			William Bob	William	B		
4	Bob	Jay	William	Bob, William			Edward Isaac	Edward			
5	McSmith	G	Gilbert	McSmith, Gilbert			Jason Harold	Jason			
6	John	Kelly	Mills	John, Mills							
7	Harold	H	Jason	Harold, Jason							
8	Isaac	M	Edward	Isaac, Edward							
9	Luky		James	Lucky, James							
10	Smith	F	Harry	Smith, Harry							
11	Carl	P	Marx	Carl, Marx							
12											

We can use Flash Fill for numbers and add some pattern to the numbers. For instance, we have a set of phone numbers in our database that we want to insert the first three numbers in a bracket and also add a dash in between the number. We can use Flash Fill to add these patterns to all the phone numbers in the database automatically.

PHONE NUMBERS

5521299210	(552)129-9210
2239820123	(223)982-0123
5629827823	(562)982-7823
7179820144	(717)982-0144
5159825124	(515)982-5124
1129890100	(112)989-0100
5059120321	(505)912-0321
3844822109	(384)482-2109
9199330131	(919)933-0131
4459829144	(445)982-9144

Hit the Enter key on the keyboard to accept the suggestions.

PHONE NUMBERS

5521299210	(552)129-9210
2239820123	(223)982-0123
5629827823	(562)982-7823
7179820144	(717)982-0144
5159825124	(515)982-5124
1129890100	(112)989-0100
5059120321	(505)912-0321
3844822109	(384)482-2109
9199330131	(919)933-0131
4459829144	(445)982-9144

Duplicating Content of a Cell

If you want to duplicate the content of a cell, instead of clicking and dragging using the AutoFill handle or copying and pasting, you can select the cell below it and use the shortcut key Ctrl+D and it duplicates whatever is in the cell above. This works for text and does not work very well for numbers.

Text to Column

The Text to Column feature breaks up phrases or groups of words in a cell into their separate cells. In other words, the Text to Column feature split a single column of text into multiple columns. For instance, you can separate a column of full names into separate first and last name columns. You can also choose how to split it up – Fixed width or split at each comma, period, or other characters. To illustrate this, let's utilize our Midas Concept Payroll below:

	A	B	C	D	E	F	G
25							
26			**Midas Concept LLC**				
27			Payroll				
28	Employee	Name	Social Security Numb	Date of Employm	Hour	Rate	Gross
29	2437110	Mark, Spencer	450012432	1/22/2019	50	$75.00	$3,000.00
30	2437111	John, Bolt	341112434	7/24/2019	50	$44.30	$1,772.00
31	2437112	James, Phrase	670022435	2/24/2018	52	$19.90	$835.00
32	2437113	Luther , Miles	882012539	6/3/2017		$15.00	$0.00
33	2437114	Harry, Cliton	553112632	12/28/2019		$55.50	$0.00
34	2437115	Bells, Simpson	125512442	1/5/2017	45	$12.00	$430.00
35	2437116	Bob, Kelly	5220012489	8/23/2019	45	$12.00	$430.00
36	2437117	Martins, April	538012498	8/13/2018		$15.50	$0.00
37	2437118	James, Kingsley	587012489	9/27/2018	30	$49.00	$1,960.00
38	2437119	Robert, Hume	480026440	10/7/2019	30	$55.95	$1,808.00
39	2437120	Harold, Jason	552812450	8/30/2019	30	$45.20	$1,920

We shall break the name column up so we have separate cells for each name (Last Name and First Name) using the Text-to-Column feature. We can't put the broken up names in the next column because it will overwrite the social security numbers. So what we do is to right-click on the column

111

header next to the column we intend to break up. In this case, the column header is Column C. So we right-click on the column header C and click on "Insert"

	A	B	C		D	E	F	G
25				Cut				
26				Copy	idas Concept LLC			
27		Right-Click on C		Paste Options:	Payroll			
28	**Employee**	**Name**	**Social Se**	Paste Special...	te of Employm	Hour	Rate	Gross
29	2437110	Mark, Spencer		Insert	1/22/2019	50	$75.00	$3,000.00
30	2437111	John, Bolt		Delete	7/24/2019	50	$44.30	$1,772.00
31	2437112	James, Phrase		Clear Contents	2/24/2018	52	$19.90	$835.00
32	2437113	Luther , Miles		Format Cells...	6/3/2017		$15.00	$0.00
33	2437114	Harry, Cliton		Column Width...	12/28/2019		$55.50	$0.00
34	2437115	Bells, Simpson		Hide	1/5/2017	45	$12.00	$430.00
35	2437116	Bob, Kelly	5220012489	Unhide	8/23/2019	45	$12.00	$430.00
36	2437117	Martins, April	538012498		8/13/2018		$15.50	$0.00
37	2437118	James, Kingsley	587012489		9/27/2018	30	$49.00	$1,960.00
38	2437119	Robert, Hume	480026440		10/7/2019	30	$55.95	$1,808.00
39	2437120	Harold, Jason	552812450		8/30/2019	30	$45.20	$1,920

This action pushes the content one step away, so it doesn't get overwritten. That is, the content of column C is moved to column D to create an empty column.

	A	B	C	D	E	F	G	H
25								
26					**Midas Concept LLC**			
27					Payroll			
28	**Employee**	**Name**		Social Security Numb	Date of Employm	Hour	Rate	Gross
29	2437110	Mark, Spencer		450012432	1/22/2019	50	$75.00	$3,000.00
30	2437111	John, Bolt		341112434	7/24/2019	50	$44.30	$1,772.00
31	2437112	James, Phrase		670022435	2/24/2018	52	$19.90	$835.00
32	2437113	Luther , Miles		882012539	6/3/2017		$15.00	$0.00
33	2437114	Harry, Cliton		553112632	12/28/2019		$55.50	$0.00
34	2437115	Bells, Simpson	Content of Column	125512442	1/5/2017	45	$12.00	$430.00
35	2437116	Bob, Kelly	C Is Pushed to	5220012489	8/23/2019	45	$12.00	$430.00
36	2437117	Martins, April	Column D	538012498	8/13/2018		$15.50	$0.00
37	2437118	James, Kingsley		587012489	9/27/2018	30	$49.00	$1,960.00
38	2437119	Robert, Hume		480026440	10/7/2019	30	$55.95	$1,808.00
39	2437120	Harold, Jason		552812450	8/30/2019	30	$45.20	$1,920

- Next, select the range of data you wish to break up (in this case, Name of Employees)
- Click on the "Data" tab
- Go to the Data Tools Group
- Click on "Text to Column."

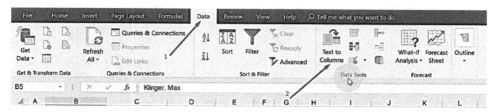

- This opens up a wizard.

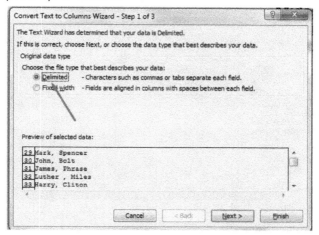

Select "Delimited." The Delimiter used in separating the First Names from the Last Name in our data is Comma> click on "NEXT" > Check the box next to Comma. This action separates the Last Names from the First Name with a vertical line.

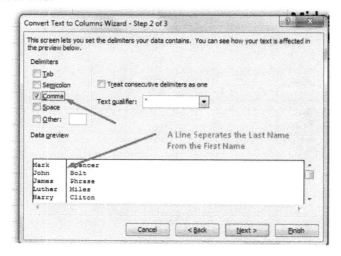

But you will notice that we have space to the right-hand side of the comma or the vertical line. To get rid of the space, check the box next to "space" and it collapses the space between the line and the last name.

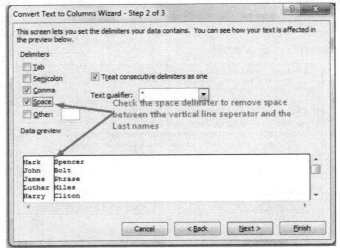

Click "Next" to set up the data format for the First Name column or the Last Name column. The options include General, or you want it to be text, date, or you want to skip importing the column. Leave this at "General."

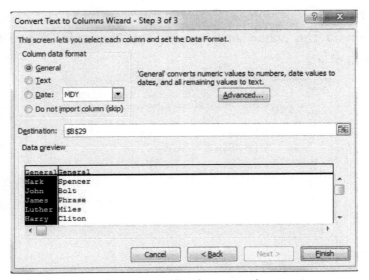

Select the column you wish to move to the new destination

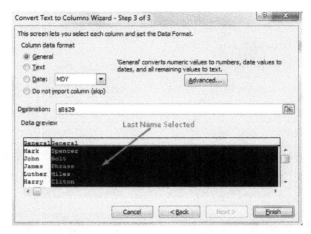

Finally, select the column that contains the Names (in this illustration, column B) and click "Finish" this will dump the last name in the next available column.

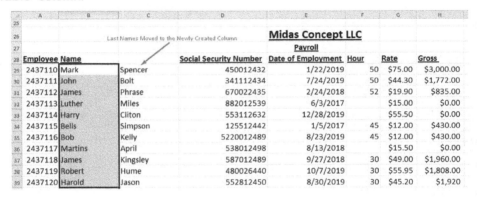

You can now update the title of the Name columns to First and Last Name.

Employee	First Name	Last Name	Social Security Number	Date of Employment	Hour	Rate	Gross
			Midas Concept LLC				
			Payroll				
2437110	Mark	Spencer	450012432	1/22/2019	50	$75.00	$3,000.00
2437111	John	Bolt	341112434	7/24/2019	50	$44.30	$1,772.00
2437112	James	Phrase	670022435	2/24/2018	52	$19.90	$835.00
2437113	Luther	Miles	882012539	6/3/2017		$15.00	$0.00
2437114	Harry	Cliton	553112632	12/28/2019		$55.50	$0.00
2437115	Bells	Simpson	125512442	1/5/2017	45	$12.00	$430.00
2437116	Bob	Kelly	5220012489	8/23/2019	45	$12.00	$430.00
2437117	Martins	April	538012498	8/13/2018		$15.50	$0.00
2437118	James	Kingsley	587012489	9/27/2018	30	$49.00	$1,960.00
2437119	Robert	Hume	480026440	10/7/2019	30	$55.95	$1,808.00
2437120	Harold	Jason	552812450	8/30/2019	30	$45.20	$1,920

Editing Data

Editing Cells, Columns and Rows

You can move the contents of a column by simply right-clicking on the column header and selecting "Insert." You can also move contents of a row downwards to create a new row above by right-clicking on the row header and clicking on "Insert." In addition to this, you can delete cells, sheet rows, sheet columns and entire Excel sheet by highlighting any of them > click on "Home," go over to the "Cell Groups" and click on the drop-down arrow by "Delete."

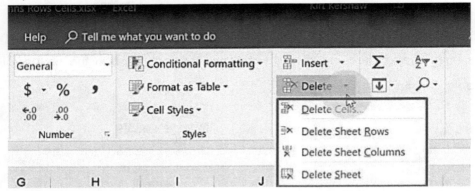

You can also use the insert option to insert cells, sheet rows, sheet columns and an entire Sheet. You could also cut the contents of a sheet and insert it in a selected section of another sheet.

Another important editing function of the cells in a sheet is the ability to Shift cells. We can shift cells right, down, or insert an entirely new row(s) or new column(s).

116

To do this, select the cell you want to shift, right-click on the mouse and select "Insert" > choose the option you want to use and click on "OK."

Find & Replace Data

To help you find or replace data on your spreadsheet, you can use the Find & Replace feature, which is found on the "Home" tab under the "Editing" group. Search for the magnifying glass icon and click on the drop-down menu by the side and select "Find." Or you can use the shortcut key "Ctrl + F."

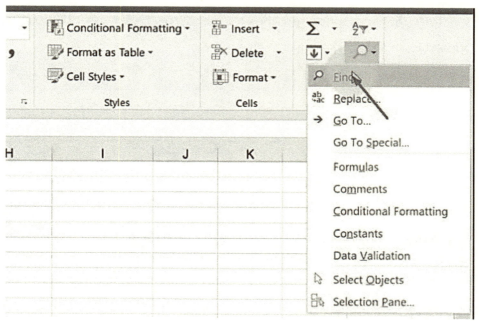

Within the "Find" dialogue box, we have the "Find" as well as the "Find and Replace" option. You can use the "Find" option to search for any item within the worksheet by typing the name of the item in the "Find what" search box and keep clicking on "Find Next" or "Find All." The "Find All" option lists all the items you are searching for and the cells they are placed.

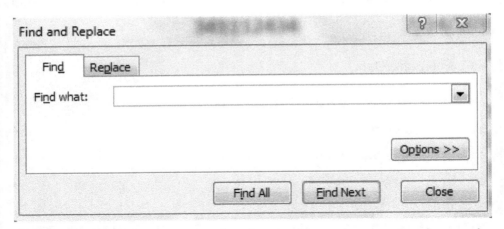

By default, the Find option searches for item(s) row by row. But this can be updated to search column by column.

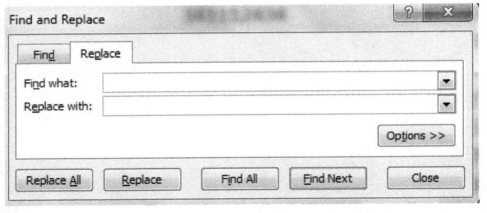

The "Find & Replace" option is used to find content(s) within the worksheet and replace these content(s) with something else. Type in the item you which to replace in the "Find what:" box. while the new item to replace the old item is keyed into the "Replace with" box. You may choose to find and replace the item(s) at once or replace them one after the other.

If you want the "Find and Replace" feature to affect several sheets, click on "Options" in the "Find and Replace" dialogue box,

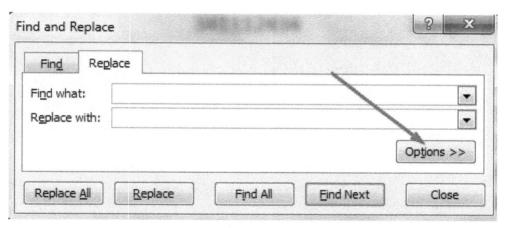

Now, instead of searching within the active sheet, we can select "Workbook" in the "Within option" and click on "Find Next" or "Find All."

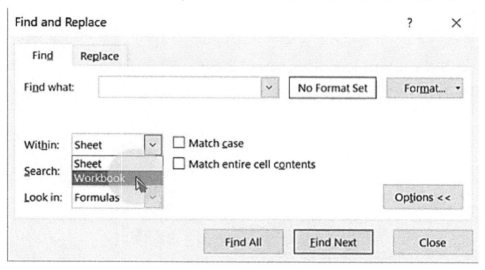

This searches the entire worksheet and adds the Find and Replace feature. Finally, there are several "Find" Formats to select. For instance, you can search for items that have particular emphasis or formatting. For example, we could narrow our search to numbers or text that is bold or written with a specific style of font, font size, font color, etc. To do this, click on the drop-down arrow next to "Format" at the top-right corner and set up the search option and set the search criteria.

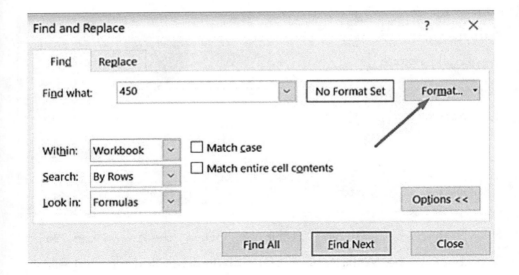

Go To Option

The Go-To feature with its shortcut key "Ctrl + G" works just like it sounds. It allows you to jump to a specific cell, page, line, footnote, comment, or other places within your document. For the Go-To feature, click on the Home tab > move to the "Editing group" > click the drop-down arrow next to the magnifying glass icon, then click on Go-To. Alternatively, you can use the F5 keys to activate it.

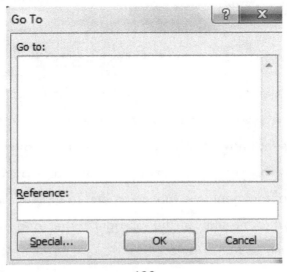

One exciting aspect of the Go-To feature is that you can type in the reference you want to go to, and it is highlighted. It also stores the last reference cell number you moved from.

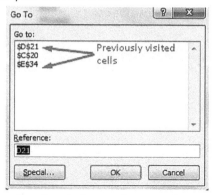

At the bottom of the Go-To dialogue box is the "Special" button. This is used to set up features the Go To option should reference. Here you can set up the Go To Special to reference comments, constants, formulas, blank cells, objects, etc. Under the "Formulas" option, you can choose between numbers, text, logical, or errors. You can also select all the options under formulas.

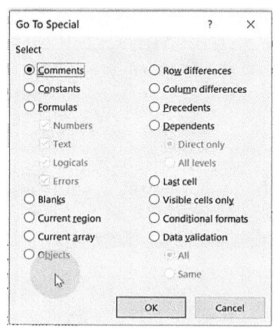

For instance, if the "Formulas" option is selected and you click the "OK" button, the Go-To feature will only highlight cells that contain formulas. When we used chose the "Formulas" option on Go To Special for our "Sales Spread Sheet" examples, the following cells with formulas where highlighted.

	H8		f_x	=SUM(C8:F8)							
	A	B	C	D	E	F	G	H	I	J	K
1	Sales Spread sheet										
2	5/15/2020										
3											
4						Commission:		8%			
5											
6		Employee ID	January	February	March	April		Total	Average	Sales Commissions	
7											
8		2437661	10110	11175.7	34141	15135		70562	17641	5644.9608	
9		2437662	22201	12210.6	21241	17206		72858	18214	5828.6392	
10		2347663	19210	15185.1	25195	12310		71901	17975	5752.0824	
11		2437664	35220	11195.4	30186	19250		95851	23963	7668.1056	
12											
13		Month Total	86741	49766.8	110763	63902					
14		Month Averag	21685	12441.7	27691	15975					
15											
16		Lowest (MIN)	10110	11175.7	21241	12310					
17		Highest (MAX)	35220	15185.1	34141	19250					
18											

To verify if these cells contain formulas, we use the shortcut key below to confirm:

CTRL + ~

When we do that, the formulas in each cell is revealed.

	H8		f_x	=SUM(C8:F8)					
	B	C	D	E	F	G	H	I	J
1									
2									
3									
4					Commission:		0.08		
5									
6	Employee ID	January	February	March	April		Total	Average	Sales Commissions
7									
8	2437661	10110.25	11175.65	34140.96	15135.15		=SUM(C8:F8)	=AVERAGE(C8:F8	=H8*H4
9	2437662	22200.75	12210.63	21240.82	17205.79		=SUM(C9:F9)	=AVERAGE(C9:F9	=H9*H4
10	2347663	19210.34	15185.11	25195.14	12310.44		=SUM(C10:F10)	=AVERAGE(C10:F	=H10*H4
11	2437664	35220.15	11195.37	30185.66	19250.14		=SUM(C11:F11)	=AVERAGE(C11:F	=H11*H4
12									
13	Month Total	=C8+C9+C10+C1	=D8+D9+D10+D11	=E8+E9+E10+E11	=F8+F9+F10+F1				
14	Month Average	=C13/4	=D13/4	=E13/4	=F13/4				
15									
16	Lowest (MIN)	=MIN(C8:C11)	=MIN(D8:D11)	=MIN(E8:E11)	=MIN(F8:F11)				
17	Highest (MAX)	=MAX(C8:C11)	=MAX(D8:D11)	=MAX(E8:E11)	=MAX(F8:F11)				
18									
19									

Use the same shortcut key to return it to numbers.

Transpose Data

To transpose your data, that is, to take a range of data and flip it, select the range of data you wish to transpose or flip and copy them (Ctrl + C). Go ahead and pick a blank cell away from the data, so you don't accidentally paste it over any other data. To paste it, go to the Home Tab under the Clipboard group and click on the paste drop-down arrow and click on the "Transpose" option.

We can illustrate this by using our "Sales Spread Sheet." Now, let's transpose the column for Employee ID, January, February, March and April with their corresponding content. The first thing we should do is to highlight everything we intend to transpose.

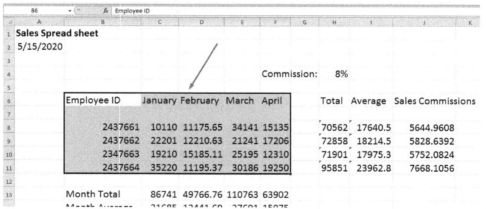

Next step, we copy the highlighted cells (Ctrl + C). After copying the cells, we click on an empty cell far away from where there are data.

Next, click on "Home" tab > under the Clipboard section locate "Paste" > Click on the drop-down arrow under the "Paste" icon > locate "Transpose" and click on it.

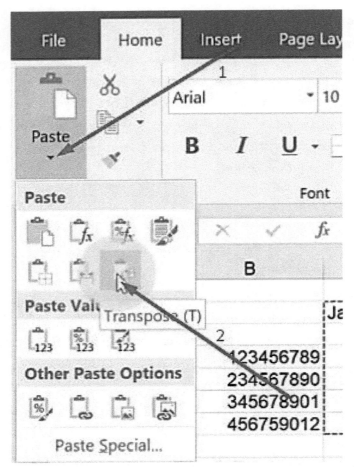

After hitting the Transpose button, the selected cell range and its contents are transposed or flipped from the top to the side

	A	B	C	D	E	F	G	H
16		Lowest (MIN)	10110.3	11175.65	21240.82	12310.44		
17		Highest (MAX)	35220.2	15185.11	34140.96	19250.14		
18								
19								
20								
21								
22		Employee ID		2437661	2437662	2347663	2437664	
23		January		10110.25	22200.75	19210.34	35220.15	
24		February		11175.65	12210.63	15185.11	11195.37	
25		March		34140.96	21240.82	25195.14	30185.66	
26		April		15135.15	17205.79	12310.44	19250.14	
27								
28								
29								
30								

Another way to transpose data is with the aid of the function "Transpose." To use the **TRANSPOSE Function** option, select a range of the same proportion you want to be transposed. For instance, if we wish to transpose the cell range Employee ID, January, February, March and April, we will select them, including the data beneath them. In our example, we have five columns and five rows, so we move to a space outside the data area and highlight five rows and five columns of empty cells.

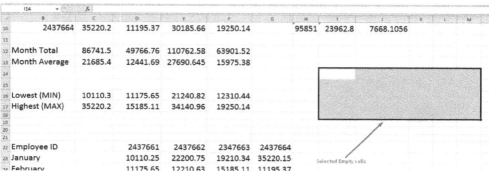

Next, type in the Transpose Function in the outer cell of the highlighted cells. Type in "equal TRANSPOSE bracket open, then highlight the range of Cells you wish to transpose and then close the bracket."

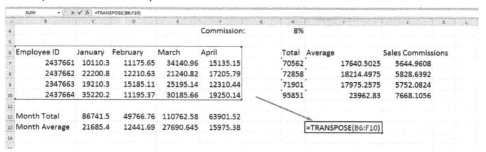

Note that you won't hit the ENTER key on the keyboard to activate the Transpose Function; instead, you will hold down on the Control key plus the Shift key and hit the Enter Key.

Ctrl+Shift+Enter

This automatically transposes the selected data range.

The transpose option does better with text and data, but when it comes to functions and formulas, not so much because data resulting from formulas require cell referencing and any flipping alters the data.

AutoFormat Feature

The auto-format feature contains a gallery of predefined formats that you can apply to a range of cells in a single click. For instance, in our "Sales Spread Sheet," we can modify our data range by offsetting the column labels with some fill colors, a different type of fonts, as well as modify the row labels, add a number format for the sales numbers of all employees, etc. by selecting it.

	A	B	C	D	E	F	G	H	I
	B6			fx	Employee ID				
1	Sales Spread sheet								
2	5/15/2020			Our Mini Database is Highlighted to apply AutoFormat feature					
3									
4						Commission:		8%	
5									
6		Employee ID	January	February	March	April		Total	Average
7		2437661	10110.3	11175.65	34140.96	15135.15		70562	17640.5025
8		2437662	22200.8	12210.63	21240.82	17205.79		72858	18214.4975
9		2347663	19210.3	15185.11	25195.14	12310.44		71901	17975.2575
10		2437664	35220.2	11195.37	30185.66	19250.14		95851	23962.83
11									
12		Month Total	86741.5	49766.76	110762.58	63901.52			
13		Month Average	21685.4	12441.69	27690.645	15975.38			

We can see what options are available for us in the AutoFormat gallery by adding it to the Quick Access Toolbar. To do this, click on the Quick Access Toolbar > "Customize Quick Access Toolbar" > click on the drop-down arrow in the "Choose Command from" menu and select the "All Commands" Option.

Next, scroll down to where you have "AutoFormat" and double-click on it to add it to the right-hand side. Finally, Click "OK" to add it to the Quick Access Toolbar. Now, with our mini database selected, click on the AutoFormat icon on the Quick Access Menu, and this will bring up several AutoFormat options to choose from.

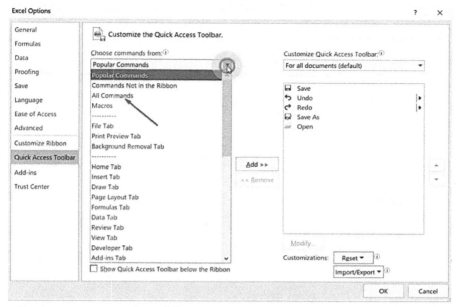

Scroll down to see the different design options that are available to choose from to modify the selected section of your spreadsheet you wish to modify.

Click "OK" to apply your modification choice. At the base of the AutoFormat dialogue box is the "Options" button which gives us options for data to be exempted from the AutoFormat modification within our selected cell range, For instance, we can choose not to apply the modification to either numbers, Borders, fonts, patterns, alignments, width and height within the selected range of cells.

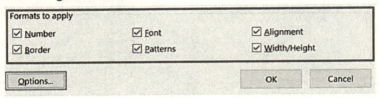

Chapter Seven
Conditional Formatting

Basic Conditional Formatting

Conditional formatting allows you to automatically apply formatting such as colors, icons, and data bars to one or more cells based on the cell value. The conditional formatting feature will apply formatting to cells when a certain condition has been met. To do this, you'll need to create a conditional formatting rule which must be met. To fulfill these conditions, let's select a range of cells from our spreadsheet called "Book Sales For The Year."

	A	B	C	D	E	F	G	H	I	J	K	L	M	N
1						BOOK SALES FOR THE YEAR								
2	BOOK TYPE	JAN	FEB	MAR	APR	MAY	JUNE	JULY	AUG	SEPT	OCT	NOV	DEC	YEAR TOTAL
3	HEALTH BOOKS	130,000	200,000	280,000	260,000	150,000	200,000	350,000	150,000	150,000	250,000	350,000	450,000	2,920,000
4	FICTION	100,000	180,000	350,000	350,000	150,000	150,000	280,000	350,000	300,000	350,000	350,000	400,000	3,310,000
5	COOKBOOKS	150,000	250,000	250,000	300,000	150,000	180,000	280,000	150,000	150,000	350,000	280,000	400,000	2,890,000
6	TOTAL BOOKS	380,000	630,000	880,000	910,000	450,000	530,000	910,000	650,000	600,000	950,000	980,000	1,250,000	9,120,000
7														

In this illustration, we have a record of different book genres sold (in hundred of thousands) in a year and the total amount sold. Let's say we want to identify those months where the books sold are greater than 250,000. To do this, we apply a format in the conditional formatting rule that meets this condition. First, we select our range of cells that contains all the conditions.

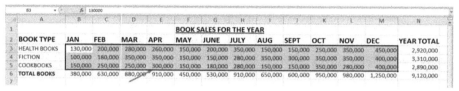

Next, go to the "Styles" group under the Home Tab and Click on "Conditional Formatting."

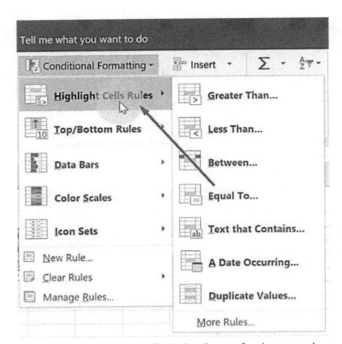

When we select the "Highlight Cells Rules," you find several conditions that can be applied. For instance Greater than, Less than, between, Equal to, etc. Since, in our example, we are looking for cells within our range of cells with values greater than 250,000, we will click on the "Greater than" option. This brings up the Greater than dialogue box where we type in our conditions and the colors to highlight the cells that meet our condition(s).

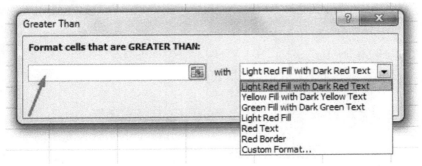

We then type in 250,000 as our conditional value and select the drop-down menu to choose colors to fill the cells. In this illustration, we use

"Yellow Fill with Dark Yellow Text." Finally, click the "OK" button to apply the condition to your range of cells.

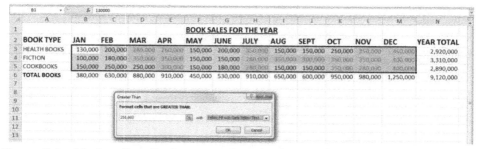

This will highlight all cells that met the condition of greater than 250,000 and fill them with yellow while the text within the cells is changed to dark yellow.

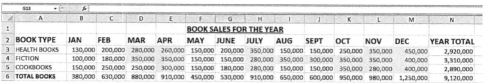

You can fill the cells with any color or change the text color or border colors. You can also choose to do your custom format by selecting your font color, border color and fill color. To customize your cells in conditional formatting, click "Custom Format" from the drop-down menu.

We can make a conditional statement for sales that rank so low, let's say cells with sales below 25% of the selected range. To do this, we highlight the range > click on 'Conditional Statement' > 'To or Bottom Rules' > Bottom 10%. Although it says Bottom 10%, you can change the percentage from 10 to any value. In this case, we are using 25%.

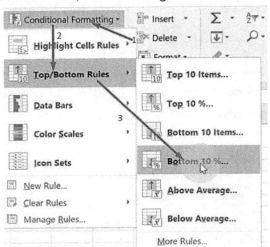

Click 'OK' to finish.

	A	B	C	D	E	F	G	H	I	J	K	L	M	N
1							BOOK SALES FOR THE YEAR							
2	BOOK TYPE	JAN	FEB	MAR	APR	MAY	JUNE	JULY	AUG	SEPT	OCT	NOV	DEC	YEAR TOTAL
3	HEALTH BOOKS	130,000	200,000	280,000	260,000	150,000	200,000	350,000	150,000	150,000	250,000	350,000	450,000	2,920,000
4	FICTION	100,000	180,000	350,000	350,000	150,000	150,000	280,000	350,000	300,000	350,000	350,000	400,000	3,310,000
5	COOKBOOKS	150,000	250,000	250,000	300,000	150,000	180,000	280,000	150,000	150,000	350,000	280,000	400,000	2,890,000
6	TOTAL BOOKS	380,000	630,000	880,000	910,000	450,000	530,000	910,000	650,000	600,000	950,000	980,000	1,250,000	9,120,000

Another feature of the Conditional Statement is the addition of data bars to represent values in our cells. The higher the value within the cell, the longer the data bar. There are several data bar options we can choose from. For instance, if we choose 'Gradient,' we have bars with different colors representing data within the cells typically fades out from a solid to a lighter shade at the tip. The 'Solid Fill' option for data bars represents values within cells with a bold color, which varies in length depending on the size of the values each cell holds. To illustrate this, let's apply data bars to the "Book Sales For the Year" Spreadsheet.

- Highlight the range of cells
- Click on Conditional Formatting
- Select Data Bars
- Select between Gradient fill or solid fill.

BOOK TYPE	JAN	FEB	MAR	APR	MAY	JUNE	JULY	AUG	SEPT	OCT	NOV	DEC	YEAR TOTAL
					BOOK SALES FOR THE YEAR								
HEALTH BOOKS	130,000	200,000	280,000	260,000	150,000	200,000	350,000	150,000	150,000	250,000	350,000	450,000	2,920,000
FICTION	100,000	180,000	350,000	350,000	150,000	150,000	280,000	350,000	300,000	350,000	350,000	400,000	3,310,000
COOKBOOKS	150,000	250,000	250,000	300,000	150,000	180,000	280,000	150,000	150,000	350,000	280,000	400,000	2,890,000
TOTAL BOOKS	380,000	630,000	880,000	910,000	450,000	530,000	910,000	650,000	600,000	950,000	980,000	1,250,000	9,120,000

For the Color Scales option in Conditional Statement, instead of having bars growing, we have color change as the numbers get larger.

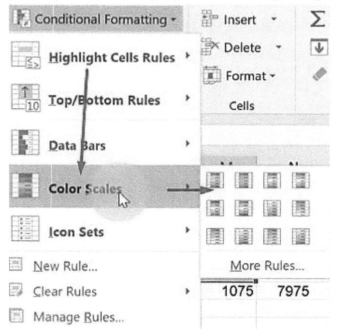

We have several color ranges; for instance, we have the Green-Yellow-Red color scale. The red represents the lower end of the scale, the yellow representing the mid-range of the scale, and the yellow representing the upper end of the scale. To apply the color scale conditional Formatting option to our illustration,

- Highlight the range of cells
- Click on 'Conditional Formatting'
- Select 'Color Scales'
- Choose between the various color scales

BOOK TYPE	JAN	FEB	MAR	APR	MAY	JUNE	JULY	AUG	SEPT	OCT	NOV	DEC	YEAR TOTAL
HEALTH BOOKS	130,000	200,000	280,000	260,000	150,000	200,000	350,000	150,000	150,000	250,000	350,000	450,000	2,920,000
FICTION	100,000	180,000	350,000	350,000	150,000	150,000	280,000	350,000	300,000	350,000	350,000	400,000	3,310,000
COOKBOOKS	150,000	250,000	250,000	300,000	150,000	180,000	280,000	150,000	150,000	350,000	280,000	400,000	2,890,000
TOTAL BOOKS	380,000	630,000	880,000	910,000	450,000	530,000	910,000	650,000	600,000	950,000	980,000	1,250,000	9,120,000

The last but not the least Conditional Formatting option is the icon Sets. Here we can represent the various data using icons to rate the lowest to the largest. For instance, we can add star ratings to the data in our Book Sales for the Year Worksheet.

To do this,

- Highlight the range of cells
- Click on Conditional Formatting
- Select icon Sets
- Click on the star rating

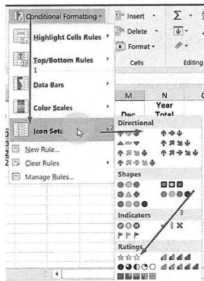

	A	B	C	D	E	F	G	H	I	J	K	L	M	N
1						BOOK SALES FOR THE YEAR								
2	BOOK TYPE	JAN	FEB	MAR	APR	MAY	JUNE	JULY	AUG	SEPT	OCT	NOV	DEC	YEAR TOT
3	HEALTH BOOKS	130,000	200,000	280,000	260,000	150,000	200,000	350,000	150,000	150,000	250,000	350,000	450,000	2,920,0
4	FICTION	100,000	180,000	350,000	350,000	150,000	150,000	280,000	350,000	300,000	350,000	350,000	400,000	3,310,0
5	COOKBOOKS	150,000	250,000	250,000	300,000	150,000	180,000	280,000	150,000	150,000	350,000	280,000	400,000	2,890,0
6	TOTAL BOOKS	380,000	630,000	880,000	910,000	450,000	530,000	910,000	650,000	600,000	950,000	980,000	1,250,000	9,120,0

You can as well apply arrows to represent data in the cells.

	A	B	C	D	E	F	G	H	I	J	K	L	M	N
1						BOOK SALES FOR THE YEAR								
2	BOOK TYPE	JAN	FEB	MAR	APR	MAY	JUNE	JULY	AUG	SEPT	OCT	NOV	DEC	YEAR TOT
3	HEALTH BOOKS	⬇ 130,000	🔽 200,000	↗ 280,000	🔽 260,000	⬇ 150,000	🔽 200,000	↗ 350,000	⬇ 150,000	⬇ 150,000	🔽 250,000	↗ 350,000	⬆ 450,000	2,920,0
4	FICTION	⬇ 100,000	🔽 180,000	↗ 350,000	↗ 350,000	⬇ 150,000	⬇ 150,000	↗ 280,000	↗ 350,000	↗ 300,000	↗ 350,000	↗ 350,000	⬆ 400,000	3,310,0
5	COOKBOOKS	⬇ 150,000	🔽 250,000	🔽 250,000	↗ 300,000	⬇ 150,000	⬇ 180,000	↗ 280,000	⬇ 150,000	⬇ 150,000	↗ 350,000	↗ 280,000	⬆ 400,000	2,890,0
6	TOTAL BOOKS	380,000	630,000	880,000	910,000	450,000	530,000	910,000	650,000	600,000	950,000	980,000	1,250,000	9,120,0

We can clear the conditional formatting highlighting of selected cells by highlighting the cell range > go to the 'Home' tab and click on 'Conditional Formatting' then go down to 'Clear Rules' > 'Clear Rules from Entire Cells.' You could also select 'Clear Rules from Entire Sheets' if you wish to get rid of all conditional formatting within your worksheet.

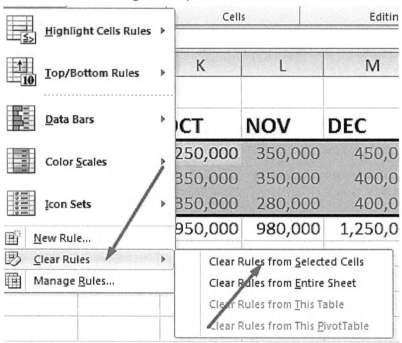

The 'Manage Rule' option allows us to create, edit, delete, and view all conditional formatting rules in the workbooks by using the conditional formatting rules manager. You can select the conditional formatting rules in a worksheet or several worksheets and delete them instead of using the

135

clear rules from selected cells or clear rules from the entire sheet. This way, only selected rules will be deleted with the aid of the manager, then click 'Apply.' You can also use the conditional formatting rules manager to give precedence on what icon sets should be placed above which. Another application for the Conditional Formatting Rules Manager is the application of different Conditional Format to different cell range. This way, you may use an icon set for the sales and Data bars for the total amount of sales. You could use different icon sets for the different genres of books and color scales for the total or any way you think is suitable for your data. You could also edit the formatting rule from the rule manager. For instance, you could edit the star icon set and determine the range of numbers that should represent a star with full color, half-color, or no color.

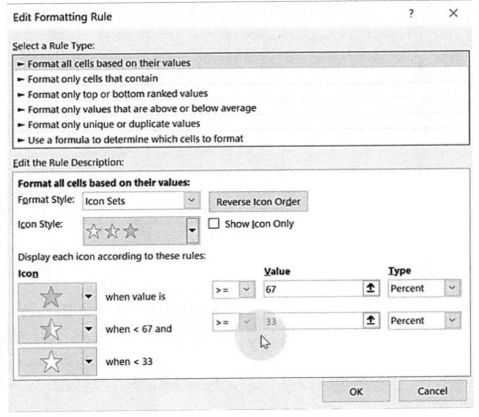

Split WorkSheet

If there ever comes, a time when you want to compare one section of your worksheet to another section and the sections you wish to compare are far apart with several columns or row between them. Instead of hiding these rows or columns in-between them, you can use the Split Worksheet option. This enables you to see both parts of the data. To do this,

- Click on the 'View Tab'
- Go over to the 'Window' group and click on 'Split.'

The split option divides the window into different panes that are scrolled separately.

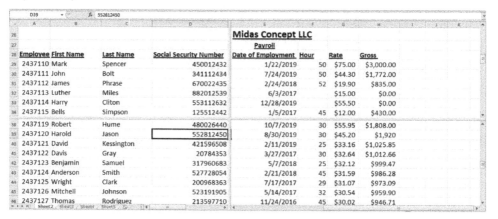

Before you click the 'Split' option, be mindful of the cell you are in because it will split the screen above and to the left of your current cell, so you have four separate quadrants, and they each scroll separately.

You can readjust your split by hovering over the inner intersection of the split borders until the cursor turns black ⬌. You can then click and drag that intersection at the center to adjust it. Let go of the cursor when you are done adjusting it. To get rid of the split-screen, hover your cursor at the intersection and double-click fast. Alternatively, you can get rid of the split by clicking on the 'View' tab and then 'Spilt' to deselect or deactivate it. You can also remove the vertical or horizontal split to have the window split into two halves – Up and down or having the window spilt into left and right instead of the four quadrants. This can be done by simply double-clicking on the vertical or horizontal split. To get rid of the vertical split, hover the cursor on the vertical split until you see arrows pointing at opposite directions then double click really fast,

54321	05/28/96
52963	06/08/05
54987	10/31/94
56789	05/30/93
85898	12/17/98
46798	06/21/85
46978	07/19/04
78956	02/15/82
57878	11/12/92

This step is also used to remove the horizontal split, so you can compare data on the left and right.

Freeze Panes

To freeze a portion of the worksheet so that it remains visible as you scroll, you can use the freeze panes feature. In other words, the Freeze Panes freezes a portion of the sheet to keep it visible while you navigate through the rest of the sheet. This feature is useful for checking out data (or comparing data) in other parts of your worksheet without losing your headers or labels. Before you activate the freeze panes, you need to be mindful of what cell is selected, because when you activate it, it will freeze everything above and left of that cell. You won't be able to scroll those parts of the worksheet. To activate the freeze panes feature,

- Go to the 'Vie' tab
- Under the window group, click on 'Freeze Panes'

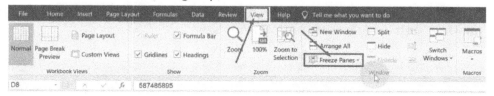

- On the drop-down menu that pops up, select freeze pane

Freeze Panes
Keep rows and columns visible while the rest of the worksheet scrolls (based on current selection).

Freeze Top Row
Keep the top row visible while scrolling through the rest of the worksheet.

Freeze First Column
Keep the first column visible while scrolling through the rest of the worksheet.

If you look at the Freeze panes icon in the drop-down menu, you will notice that there is a cell shaded in blue, which the active cell and some cells above it and on the left, which is shaded. These portions represent cells that will be frozen (static) when 'Freeze panes' is activated, and it goes along with you, wherever you scroll. To unfreeze panes, go back to the view tab and click on 'Unfreeze Panes.'

The other two options you get are the 'Freeze Top Row' and 'Freeze First Column.' Here, the top row is 'Row 1' also known as the header row and the first column is 'Column A' The 'freeze top row' option keeps the top row in-sight while you scroll through the worksheet. The 'Freeze Top Row' option is ideal for people who create databases because they put all their labels in the top row. Freezing the first row enable database administrators to compare data within the worksheet and their labels in the first row. The 'Freeze First Column' option keeps the first column static while you scroll through the entire worksheet. This is also the 'Freeze panes' option for comparing data within a worksheet.

Viewing Multi Worksheets and Workbooks

You can open up additional Excel windows to enable you to work at different places at the same time. To illustrate this, we have several worksheets with different titles – Midas Concept Payroll, Sales Commission for Midas, Contacts and Book Sales for the Year as shown below;

	H44		*fx*	973.090909090909	
	A	B	C	D	E
26					**Midas Concept**
27					**Payroll**
28	**Employee**	**First Name**	**Last Name**	**Social Security Number**	**Date of Employment**
29	2437110	Mark	Spencer	450012432	1/22/2019
30	2437111	John	Bolt	341112434	7/24/2019
31	2437112	James	Phrase	670022435	2/24/2018
32	2437113	Luther	Miles	882012539	6/3/2017
33	2437114	Harry	Cliton	553112632	12/28/2019
34	2437115	Bells	Simpson	125512442	1/5/2017
35	2437116	Bob	Kelly	522001248	8/23/2019
36	2437117	Martins	April	538012498	8/13/2018
37	2437118	James	Kingsley	587012489	9/27/2018
38	2437119	Robert	Hume	480026440	10/7/2019
39	2437120	Harold	Jason	552812450	8/30/2019
40	2437121	David	Kessington	421596508	2/11/2019
41	2437122	Davis	Gray	20784353	3/27/2017
42	2437123	Benjamin	Samuel	317960683	5/7/2018
43	2437124	Anderson	Smith	527728054	2/21/2018

Midas Concept Payroll | Sales Commission for Midas | Contacts | Book Sales for the Year

We want to be able to view all these worksheets at the same time. To do this,

- Click on the 'View' tab

- Go to the Window Group
- Select 'New Window'

The 'New Window' option will open a second window for your document so you can work in different places at the same time.

We have four worksheets; we wish to open at the same time, so click on 'New Window' four times to open four different windows of the active worksheet.

Next,

- Click on the 'View' Tab,
- Under the Window group, click on "Arrange All." 'Arrange All' option stacks your open window so you can see all of them at once.
- A dialogue box pops up for you to choose your arrangement style – Tiled, Horizontal, Vertical, and Cascade. For this illustration, we will select 'Tiled.'

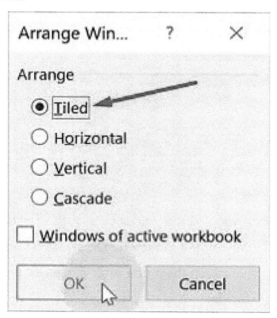

- Click 'OK'

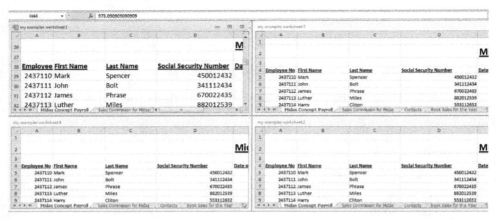

Clicking on 'OK' arranges the worksheets in a tiled format, now we can select the different worksheet titles in the various windows to see them. For instance, we could open the Midas Concept Payroll worksheet on the first window, Contacts worksheet in the second window, Sales Commission for Midas in the third window, and Book Sales for the Year Worksheet on the fourth window.

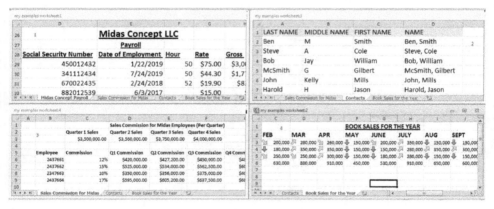

This way, we can view all the worksheets at the same time and be able to compare and contrast the data on the different worksheets. To exit the multiple windows, click on them one after the other and click the close icon at the top-right corner.

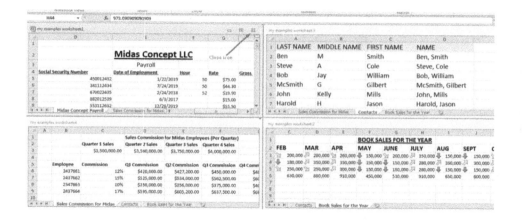

Speak Cells

Trying to compare an Excel printout with the data on the screen can be quite daunting. Most people have complained of feeling dizzy when carrying out such back and forth eye movements. You can concentrate on the printout while excel reads out the figures for you with the of the speaking cells function. This way, you don't have to keep looking at the screen and your printout. To activate the speak cells function;

- Click anywhere on the Quick Access Toolbar."
- Scroll down to "Customize the Quick Access Toolbar"
- Change it from 'Popular Commands' to 'All Commands'
- Scroll down to where the letter S begins and search for 'Speak cells'
- Select the 'Speak Cells' and click 'Add' to move it to the right-hand side. There are other Speak Cells options you can add to the Quick Access Toolbar- Stop Speaking Cells, Speak cells by Column, Speak Cells by Row, and Speak Cells on Enter.

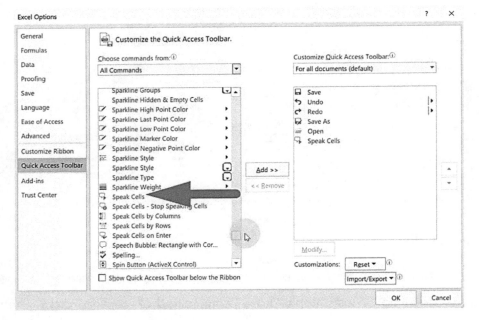

- Now, select the range of cells you want 'speak cells' to read back to you and then click on the Speak Cells icon on the Quick Access Toolbar.

- Hit the 'Esc' key on the keyboard to stop Speaking Cells and the active cell, the cell in white is where speak cells left off. If you want to continue from where you left off, go ahead and click on Speak Cells and it will resume reading the data out loud.

Sound Effects

New to Excel 2019 is the Sound Feedback feature, which provides sound effects. Sound effects can enhance your productivity in Excel by providing Audio Cues. For instance, a sound cue might notify you when the options on the screen change or a sound can confirm that an action like copying, pasting, formatting, etc. is completed. To turn the Sound cue feature ON,

- Click on 'File'

- Scroll down to 'Options'
- Click on the 'Ease of Access' Category
- Under 'Feedback options' check 'Provide feedback with sound.'

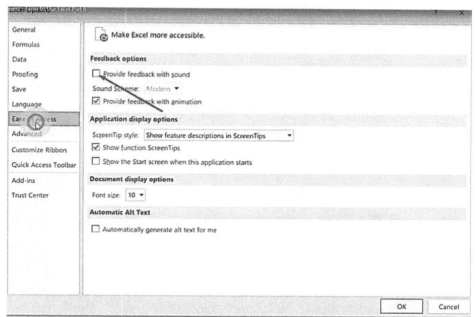

- We have the option to choose a sound scheme - modern or classic sounds.
- Click 'OK'

With sound effect activated, when you perform actions like 'Save,' 'copying & Pasting,' you will hear a sound. Note that turning ON Sound effect affects all Microsoft Office Applications (Words, Access, etc.).

Accessibility Checker

The Accessibility Checker checks the workbook for content that people with disabilities will find difficult to read, and new to Excel 2019 is the

145

one-click fixes accessibility issues feature. Let's find out if people with disability will find the spreadsheet below difficult to read;

To do this,

- Click on the 'Review' tab
- Click 'Check Accessibility',

This opens up the task pane over to the right of the window.

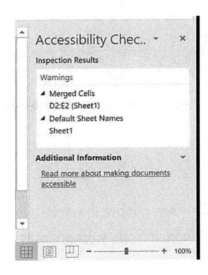

For instance, merged cells are challenging to read. To fix it and make it easy to read, hover your mouse on the warning(s) and click on the drop-down arrow and do the one-click on 'Unmerge' to unmerge it. The alert immediately disappears.

The next thing it finds would be problematic for people with disabilities to read is the fact that the worksheet is saved with its generic name 'Sheet 1.' So Excel wants us to rename the worksheet with a more specific name. To fix it, click on the drop-down arrow, and you will see where it says 'Rename sheet.'

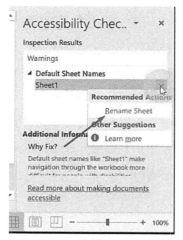

This changes the worksheet name to edit mode. We can now change the generic name to a more specific name and hit the ENTER key on the keyboard to apply it changes. You get an inspection result "No accessibility issues found. People with disabilities should not have difficulty reading this workbook" after all issues have been fixed. This way, all the accessibility issues are cleared off, making our worksheet now easy to read by people with disabilities.

Translate

Also available in Microsoft Excel 2019 is the translate feature. With this feature, we can translate selected text into a different language. To translate a text, select it > click 'Review' and under the 'language group' click 'Translate.' This opens up the task pane on the right-hand side of the window. It detects the language it is translating from (English Language) to any of the selected languages in the "To Language" box.

Row Height, Column Width and AutoFit

You can adjust cells in terms of columns and rows with predefined measurements. If you want your entire spreadsheet to have a specific row height and column weight, click on the 'Home' tab and under the 'Cells' group, click on the drop-down arrow next to 'Format' > select the Row height and key in the measurement you want in the pop-up window. The same applies to the column width. If you want an equal row height and column width for the entire worksheet, highlight the whole worksheet > click the drop-down arrow next to 'Format' and select the AutoFit Row height as well as AutoFit Column Width.

Hiding Column(s), Row(s) and Worksheet(s)

If you wish to hide columns, let's say you are doing a presentation, and you don't want to focus on a specific column or columns, you can hide them without deleting the column(s). To do this, right-click on the column header, you intend to hide and scroll down to 'Hide,' and it collapses that specific column.

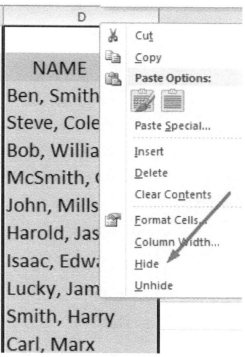

You can also do it for row(s). Highlight the row(s) you wish to hide and right-click on the header by the side, scroll to and click 'Hide' on the pop-up menu. To unhide a hidden column, select the column before it that is not hidden and the column after it > then right-click these headers and scroll to 'Unhide' and click on it. This returns the previously hidden column back. The same goes for hidden rows you wish to unhide. In addition to this, you can also hide your worksheet by right-clicking on the worksheet title and click on 'Hide.'

149

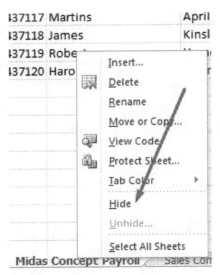

137117	Martins	April
137118	James	Kinsl
137119	Robe	
137120	Haro	

Insert...
Delete
Rename
Move or Copy...
View Code
Protect Sheet...
Tab Color ▶
Hide
Unhide...
Select All Sheets

Midas Concept Payroll   Sales Con

To unhide the worksheet, right-click on the worksheet title area and click 'Unhide' on the pop-up menu. This brings up a window with all the hidden worksheets, click on the one you wish to unhide and click 'OK.' Alternatively, you can hide your worksheet by clicking on the 'View' tab › move to the Window group and click on 'Hide' to hide the entire workbook. To unhide it, click on the 'View' tab and click on 'Unhide' from the window group.

Checking Worksheet for Spelling Errors

To check your worksheet for spelling errors, click on the 'Review' tab › go to the 'Proofing group' and select 'Spelling.'

Spelling

Alternatively, you can hit the F7 key on the keyboard to open up the spelling window. This feature selects the presumed spelling errors within your worksheet and gives you suggestions to replace such spellings. Click on 'Change' to enable Excel to replace the wrong spelling with its suggestion. The 'change all' option is used when there are several parts within the spreadsheet that misspelled text appears. This will replace the entire text with the suggested one. It also gives you an option to ignore the spelling error or 'ignore all' to ignore all the spellings errors flagged by Excel or add the flagged text into Excel's dictionary, especially when we are sure the spelling is correct.

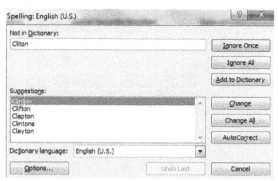

This new word is sent to Excel's custom dictionary. You can edit the custom dictionary by going to 'File' > 'Options' > 'Proofing' > 'Custom Dictionaries.'

In the 'Custom Dictionaries' dialogue box, we have the default dictionary, which is non-editable and the Custom Dictionary, which can be edited by click on 'Edit Word List.' This displays all the words you have ever added to the dictionary. You can add more words to the dictionary, delete words, or delete all dictionary additions.

Smart Lookup & Thesaurus

The Smart Lookup is used to search the content of a cell, and over in the task pane, it reveals more to explore or to define. For instance, in our 'Sales Commission For Midas employee, if we want to look up the word "Bonus."

	A	B	C	D	E	F	G	H
1				Sales Commission for Midas Employees (Per Quarter)				
2			Quarter 1 Sales	Quarter 2 Sales	Quarter 3 Sales	Quarter 4 Sales		Bonus
3			$3,500,000.00	$3,560,000.00	$3,750,000.00	$4,000,000.00		$12,000,000
4								
5		Employee	Commission	Q1 Commission	Q2 Commission	Q3 Commission	Q4 Commission	
6		2437661	12%	$420,000.00	$427,200.00	$450,000.00	$480,000.00	
7		2437662	15%	$525,000.00	$534,000.00	$562,500.00	$600,000.00	
8		2347663	10%	$350,000.00	$356,000.00	$375,000.00	$400,000.00	
9		2437664	17%	$595,000.00	$605,200.00	$637,500.00	$680,000.00	
10								

We select it and click on the 'Review' Tab > in the 'Insight group' click on 'Smart Lookup.' Alternatively, you can select the word you wish to lookup and right-click and click on 'Smart Lookup' on the menu to open up the Smart Lookup Pane on the right side of the window showing the definition as a noun, verb, and origin of the word. You also find how to pronounce a word when the speaker icon is clicked as well as explore the word on Wikipedia.

The thesaurus is used to look up synonyms, or another word that is synonymous with the word you're are looking up. So, go ahead and select the cell that contains the word you want to find a synonym for or thesaurus > click on the 'Review' tab on the menu bar > under the 'proofing' group, select 'Thesaurus.'

Thesaurus

This opens up a pane with several synonyms of the selected word on the right side of the window. You can choose any of the synonyms to replace the selected word. To do this, click on the drop-down arrow next to any of the synonym in the pane and click 'Insert.' You can also copy and paste the synonym within the Excel sheet. Keep in mind that Smart Lookup and Thesaurus works well with a single word and not a combination of words.

Basic Cell Formatting

You have the option to format cells to take whatever style you want. For instance, you can change the for style of a cell or range of cells, change the color, boldness, etc. by simply highlighting the cell(s) and click on the 'Home' tab, under the 'style' group select 'Cell styles.' This gives you a range of color fill options to apply to the selected cells.

Custom Number Format

We can add a custom number format to our data. For instance, in our 'Midas Concept LLC Payroll,' we want to add hyphens separating the numbers. The essence is to allow Excel to see it as numbers and not a combination of numbers and characters.

	Employee	First Name	Last Name	Social Security Number	Date of Employment	Hour	Rate	Gross
					Midas Concept LLC			
					Payroll			
29	2437110	Mark	Spencer	450012432	1/22/2019	50	$75.00	$3,000.00
30	2437111	John	Bolt	341112434	7/24/2019	50	$44.30	$1,772.00
31	2437112	James	Phrase	670022435	2/24/2018	52	$19.90	$835.00
32	2437113	Luther	Miles	882012539	6/3/2017		$15.00	$0.00
33	2437114	Harry	Cliton	553112632	12/28/2019		$55.50	$0.00
34	2437115	Bells	Simpson	125512442	1/5/2017	45	$12.00	$430.00
35	2437116	Bob	Kelly	522001248	8/23/2019	45	$12.00	$430.00
36	2437117	Martins	April	538012498	8/13/2018		$15.50	$0.00
37	2437118	James	Kingsley	587012489	9/27/2018	30	$49.00	$1,960.00
38	2437119	Robert	Hume	480026440	10/7/2019	30	$55.95	$1,808.00
39	2437120	Harold	Jason	552812450	8/30/2019	30	$45.20	$1,920
40	2437121	David	Kessington	421596508	2/11/2019	25	$33.16	$1,025.85
41	2437122	Davis	Gray	20784353	3/27/2017	30	$32.64	$1,012.66
42	2437123	Benjamin	Samuel	317960683	5/7/2018	25	$32.12	$999.47

First, we highlight the entire column for social security number > then right-click on the range > go down and click 'Format Cells.' This opens a 'Format Cells' dialogue box > click on 'Special.'

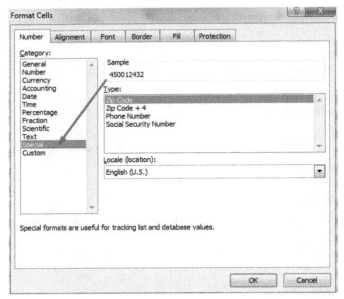

'Special' contains only four templates – 'Zip code,' 'phone number' and 'Social Security Number.'

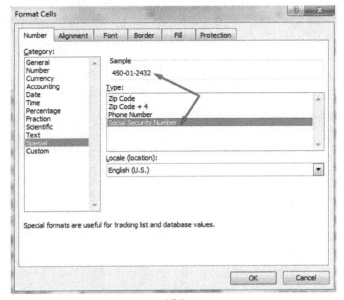

Our interest here is 'Social Security Number.' When you select 'Social Security Number,' it adds the hyphens (dash) to the sample. Then click, OK. This adds hyphens to all our social security numbers.

	A	B	C	D	E	F	G	H
25								
26				**Midas Concept LLC**				
27				Payroll				
28	Employee	First Name	Last Name	Social Security Number	Date of Employment	Hour	Rate	Gross
29	2437110	Mark	Spencer	450-01-2432	1/22/2019	50	$75.00	$3,000.00
30	2437111	John	Bolt	341-11-2434	7/24/2019	50	$44.30	$1,772.00
31	2437112	James	Phrase	670-02-2435	2/24/2018	52	$19.90	$835.00
32	2437113	Luther	Miles	882-01-2539	6/3/2017		$15.00	$0.00
33	2437114	Harry	Cliton	553-11-2632	12/28/2019		$55.50	$0.00
34	2437115	Bells	Simpson	125-51-2442	1/5/2017	45	$12.00	$430.00
35	2437116	Bob	Kelly	522-00-1248	8/23/2019	45	$12.00	$430.00
36	2437117	Martins	April	538-01-2498	8/13/2018		$15.50	$0.00
37	2437118	James	Kingsley	587-01-2489	9/27/2018	30	$49.00	$1,960.00
38	2437119	Robert	Hume	480-02-6440	10/7/2019	30	$55.95	$1,808.00
39	2437120	Harold	Jason	552-81-2450	8/30/2019	30	$45.20	$1,920
40	2437121	David	Kessington	421-59-6508	2/11/2019	25	$33.16	$1,025.85
41	2437122	Davis	Gray	020-78-4353	3/27/2017	30	$32.64	$1,012.66
42	2437123	Benjamin	Samuel	317-96-0683	5/7/2018	25	$32.12	$999.47

We could customize our social security numbers to have a text prefix, yet Excel will see it as numbers and not a combination of text and numbers. This is to prevent Excel from having trouble when we wish to apply formulas or functions to such range of cells. Now, for this illustration, we want to add 'SS' as a prefix before each social security number and want Excel to see the content of the social security number as numbers and not a combination of numbers and text. To do this, we highlight the entire Social Security Numbers > Right-Click and scroll down to 'Format Cells' > in the Format Cells dialogue box, select 'Special' under Categories > in the 'Special' category click on 'Social Security Number' > Next, Click on 'Custom' under 'Category' > under the 'Type,' key in whatever you want to prefix the social security number.

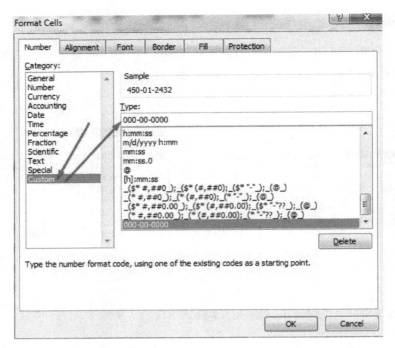

In our case, we are using 'SS.'

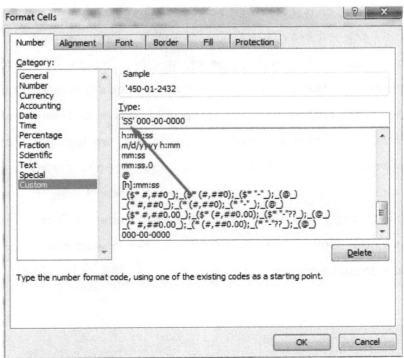

Hit the OK button to apply it.

	Employee	First Name	Last Name	Social Security Number	Date of Employment	Hour	Rate	Gross
25								
26					**Midas Concept LLC**			
27					Payroll			
28	**Employee**	**First Name**	**Last Name**	**Social Security Number**	**Date of Employment**	**Hour**	**Rate**	**Gross**
29	2437110	Mark	Spencer	SS 450012432	1/22/2019	50	$75.00	$3,000.00
30	2437111	John	Bolt	SS 341112434	7/24/2019	50	$44.30	$1,772.00
31	2437112	James	Phrase	SS 670022435	2/24/2018	52	$19.90	$835.00
32	2437113	Luther	Miles	SS 882012539	6/3/2017		$15.00	$0.00
33	2437114	Harry	Cliton	SS 553112632	12/28/2019		$55.50	$0.00
34	2437115	Bells	Simpson	SS 125512442	1/5/2017	45	$12.00	$430.00
35	2437116	Bob	Kelly	SS 522001248	8/23/2019	45	$12.00	$430.00
36	2437117	Martins	April	SS 538012498	8/13/2018		$15.50	$0.00
37	2437118	James	Kingsley	SS 587012489	9/27/2018	30	$49.00	$1,960.00
38	2437119	Robert	Hume	SS 480026440	10/7/2019	30	$55.95	$1,808.00
39	2437120	Harold	Jason	SS 552812450	8/30/2019	30	$45.20	$1,920
40	2437121	David	Kessington	SS 421596508	2/11/2019	25	$33.16	$1,025.85
41	2437122	Davis	Gray	SS 207843531	3/27/2017	30	$32.64	$1,012.66
42	2437123	Benjamin	Samuel	SS 317960683	5/7/2018	25	$32.12	$999.47

How do you know if Excel sees only the numbers and not alphabets? Click on any of the cells and look at what is displayed in the formula bar.

We can replace our prefix with something else. Let's take, for instance, we used 'SS' as our prefix, and we now desire to change it to 'SSN' instead of just 'SS.' What we do is simple,

- Bring up the 'Find' window by clicking Ctrl + F on the Keyboard

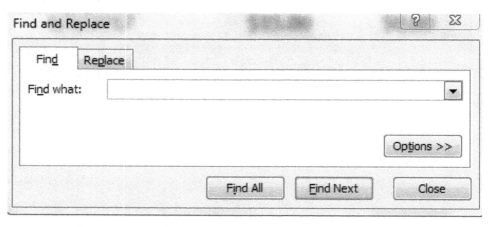

- Click on 'Options' to open it up.

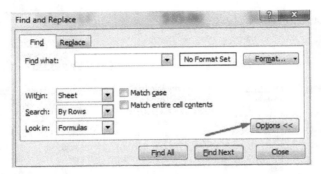

- Click on the drop-down arrow next to 'Format' to look for the specific format we wish to edit.

- We can either choose the format from the cell or click the 'Format' option. Click on the 'Format' Option, and it opens up the 'Find Format' window.

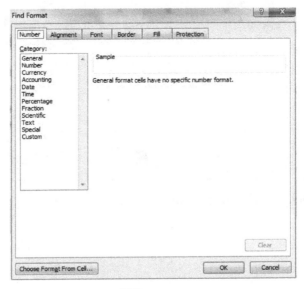

- Click on 'Custom' under the 'Category' section

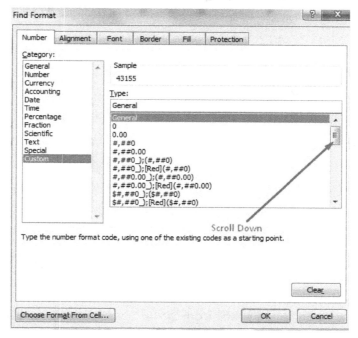

- Now scroll down until you find our custom type i.e., 'SS' 000-00-0000 and click on it.

- Click OK

- Now, Click on 'Replace' on the 'Find and Replace' window.

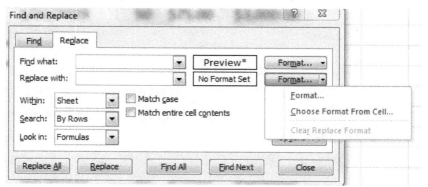

- In the 'Replace With' section, click on 'Format' to take you to the 'Replace Format' Window.

- Next, click on 'Custom' under Category and under 'Type,' scroll down and click on our previous format type 'SS' 000-00-0000. Now, Change the Prefix from 'SS' to 'SSN,' so it looks like this 'SSN' 000-00-0000

- Click OK.

- On the Find and Replace window, click on 'Find Next' when it highlights the cell with the first Social Security Number, click on 'Replace.'

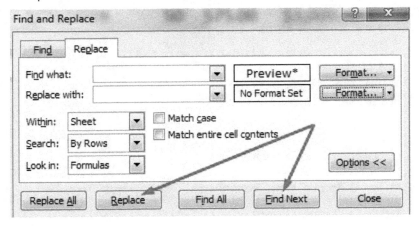

- You can also use the 'Replace All' button to replace the entire Social Security Numbers with the prefix 'SSN.'

You can apply a custom number format to cells with dates, time, zip codes, currency, numbers, etc.

Borders & Colors

You can apply borders and colors to a cell or range of cells to either make your worksheet more aesthetically pleasing to the eye or for organizational purposes, to make certain parts of your worksheet stand-out. Before we get started, the lines you see in Excel that demarcates the rows and columns are known as grid lines. The grid lines can be eliminated by clicking on the 'View' Tab › in the 'Show' group, uncheck 'Gridlines.'

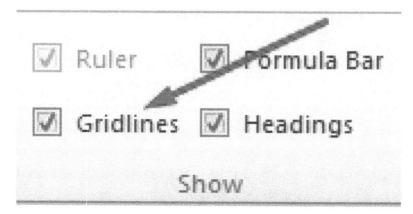

This makes your worksheet look like a regular document without those gridlines. You can turn it ON by going back to the 'View' tab and checking 'Gridlines' under the show group.' Recall that when printing Excel worksheets, the gridlines do not appear on paper. You will also notice that when we preview our worksheet, the gridlines do not show up on our print preview page. For the borders and colors, we will use our 'Sales Commission for Midas Employee' worksheet.

	A	B	C	D	E	F	G	H
1				Sales Commission for Midas Employees (Per Quarter)				
2			Quarter 1 Sales	Quarter 2 Sales	Quarter 3 Sales	Quarter 4 Sales		Bonus
3			$3,500,000.00	$3,560,000.00	$3,750,000.00	$4,000,000.00		$12,000,000
4								
5		Employee	Commission	Q1 Commission	Q2 Commission	Q3 Commission	Q4 Commission	
6		2437661	12%	$420,000.00	$427,200.00	$450,000.00	$480,000.00	
7		2437662	15%	$525,000.00	$534,000.00	$562,500.00	$600,000.00	
8		2347663	10%	$350,000.00	$356,000.00	$375,000.00	$400,000.00	
9		2437664	17%	$595,000.00	$605,200.00	$637,500.00	$680,000.00	
10								

We can choose to add a border around the headers - i.e., Employee, Commission, Q1 Commission, Q2 Commission, Q3 Commission, and Q4 Commission to make it stand out from the data below. To do this, we highlight the entire headers > click on the 'Home' tab > go to the 'Font' Group and click the border.

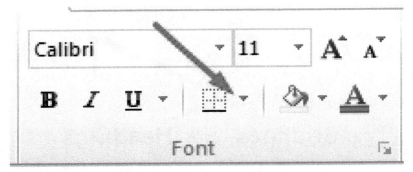

Click on the drop-down arrow to get more boarders. If you want only the bottom border to be added to your cells, click on it. You can add lines in-between the cell borders, select the 'All Borders' option to add lines in-between your boarders. You can erase specific borders by clicking on the 'Erase Border'. This adds an eraser icon to the cursor, use the cursor to click on the border you wish to erase, and it will eliminate them one cell at a time. You can remove all added borders from your cell(s) by highlighting the entire range of cells with the border and select the 'No border' option.

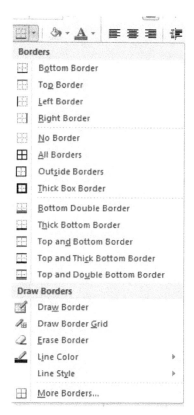

For our illustration, we want to add a thick border around the header, so we highlight the headers and select 'Thick Box Border."

Employee	Commission	Q1 Commission	Q2 Commission	Q3 Commission	Q4 Commission
2437661	12%	$420,000.00	$427,200.00	$450,000.00	$480,000.00
2437662	15%	$525,000.00	$534,000.00	$562,500.00	$600,000.00
2347663	10%	$350,000.00	$356,000.00	$375,000.00	$400,000.00
2437664	17%	$595,000.00	$605,200.00	$637,500.00	$680,000.00

This adds a thick border around the headers for our sales commission for the Midas Employee worksheet.

The 'More Borders' option gives us more cell border formatting options. Here you have several Line styles to choose from, the ability to change the border color, custom border alignments, etc.

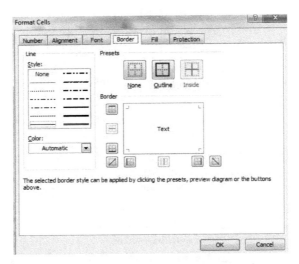

The Presets option allows you to quickly add border formats to a range of selected cells by clicking on what borderline(s) you want to be added.

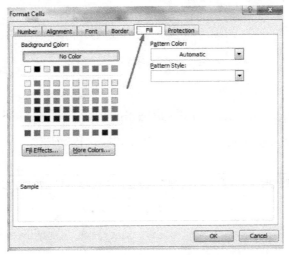

We use the fill option to add a background color to our cell or range of cells. For instance, we can fill in the range of cells holding the headers in our sales commission for Midas Employee worksheet with a background color. We highlight the range of cells, click on 'boarders in the 'Home tab' > scroll down to 'More boarders' > Fill > and select a background color and click 'OK.

	A	B	C	D	E	F	G	H
1				Sales Commission for Midas Employees (Per Quarter)				
2			Quarter 1 Sales	Quarter 2 Sales	Quarter 3 Sales	Quarter 4 Sales		Bonus
3			$3,500,000.00	$3,560,000.00	$3,750,000.00	$4,000,000.00		$12,000,000
4								
5		Employee	Commission	Q1 Commission	Q2 Commission	Q3 Commission	Q4 Commission	
6		2437661	12%	$420,000.00	$427,200.00	$450,000.00	$480,000.00	
7		2437662	15%	$525,000.00	$534,000.00	$562,500.00	$600,000.00	
8		2347663	10%	$350,000.00	$356,000.00	$375,000.00	$400,000.00	
9		2437664	17%	$595,000.00	$605,200.00	$637,500.00	$680,000.00	

'You can also choose a pattern style and a pattern color from the Fill tab. Carry out some exercises on your own and add borders and background colors to your worksheet.

Formatting Shortcuts

Let's go through some formatting shortcuts you can use when a cell is formatted and you wish to copy and apply it to another cell or a range of cells. You can use the copy and paste option.

For instance, let's select a cell (Bonus) in our "Sales Commission For Midas Employee" worksheet and carryout some formatting on this cell. First;

- We make it bold,
- Fill the cell in with yellow background-color and
- Apply a thick bottom border to it

loyees (Per Quarter)

es	Quarter 4 Sales		Bonus
00	$4,000,000.00		$12,000,000

on	Q3 Commission	Q4 Commission
00	$450,000.00	$480,000.00
00	$562,500.00	$600,000.00
00	$375,000.00	$400,000.00

165

Now, if you wish to copy this format to another cell or range of cells,

- Select the cell that contains the format you want to copy and use the shortcut key Ctrl + C to copy
- Select the cell or range of cells you want to apply the formatting to. You will need to use the formatting options because if you do a simple paste, it will bring over everything, including 'Bonus' as a text. To bring up the paste option,
- Go to the 'Home' tab
- Go to the clipboard group
- Click on the paste drop-down arrow
- Select the "Formatting" paste option.

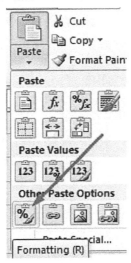

Let's paste the formatting into the column header 'Commission'

H2		fx	Bonus				
A	B	C	D	E	F	G	H
1			Sales Commission for Midas Employees (Per Quarter)				
2		Quarter 1 Sales	Quarter 2 Sales	Quarter 3 Sales	Quarter 4 Sales		Bonus
3		$3,500,000.00	$3,560,000.00	$3,750,000.00	$4,000,000.00		$12,000,000
4							
5	Employee	Commission	Q1 Commission	Q2 Commission	Q3 Commission	Q4 Commission	
6	2437661	12%	$420,000.00	$427,200.00	$450,000.00	$480,000.00	
7	2437662	15%	$525,000.00	$534,000.00	$562,500.00	$600,000.00	
8	2347663	10%	$350,000.00	$356,000.00	$375,000.00	$400,000.00	
9	2437664	17%	$595,000.00	$605,200.00	$637,500.00	$680,000.00	
10							

Alternatively, you can use the Format painter to apply a format from one cell to another cell or a range of cells. To do this,

- Select the cell you want to copy the formatting from
- Click the 'format painter' in the clipboard group under the 'Home' tab.

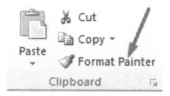

- The format painter brush enters into selection mode by converting the cursor to a cross with a brush icon next to it.
- Select a cell or click and drag across a range of cells with the format painter mode still active to apply the copied cells format. If you have a wide range of cell to apply a copied format to, go ahead and double-click the format painter brush really fast on the clipboard and the format painter mode will remain active to enable you to apply the copied format to more cells.

	A	B	C	D	E	F	G	H
1				Sales Commission for Midas Employees (Per Quarter)				
2			Quarter 1 Sales	Quarter 2 Sales	Quarter 3 Sales	Quarter 4 Sales		Bonus
3			$3,500,000.00	$3,560,000.00	$3,750,000.00	$4,000,000.00		$12,000,000
4								
5		Employee	Commission	Q1 Commission	Q2 Commission	Q3 Commission	Q4 Commission	
6		2437661	12%	$420,000.00	$427,200.00	$450,000.00	480000	
7		2437662	15%	$525,000.00	$534,000.00	$562,500.00	600000	
8		2347663	10%	$350,000.00	$356,000.00	$375,000.00	400000	
9		2437664	17%	$595,000.00	$605,200.00	$637,500.00	680000	

- Click on the ESC key to deactivate the format painter mode.

Adding Borders to Worksheet

You can add images to the background of your worksheet by

- clicking on the 'Page Layout' tab

167

- Go to the 'Page Setup' group and click on 'background.'

Background

- You can search the image from a file stored in the PC, from the search engine Bing or your OneDrive account.
- Double-click on the image to attach it to the background of your worksheet
- When you insert a background to your worksheet, when it gets to a certain region of the worksheet, the image begins to tile; in other words, it begins to repeat itself until it covers the entire worksheet.
- If you don't like the image you added to the background, go back to the 'Page Layout,' you will find 'Delete Background' under the Page Setup group. Click on it to remove the background image.

Align & Position

When it comes to aligning the content of a cell, you can do it both vertically and horizontally. In the example below, we are looking at January – December.

BOOK SALES FOR THE YEAR													
BOOK TYPE	JAN	FEB	MAR	APR	MAY	JUNE	JULY	AUG	SEPT	OCT	NOV	DEC	YEAR TOTAL
HEALTH BOOKS	130,000	200,000	280,000	260,000	150,000	200,000	350,000	150,000	150,000	250,000	350,000	450,000	2,920,000
FICTION	100,000	180,000	350,000	350,000	150,000	150,000	280,000	350,000	300,000	350,000	350,000	400,000	3,310,000
COOKBOOKS	150,000	250,000	250,000	300,000	150,000	180,000	280,000	150,000	150,000	350,000	280,000	400,000	2,890,000
TOTAL BOOKS	380,000	630,000	880,000	910,000	450,000	530,000	910,000	650,000	600,000	950,000	980,000	1,250,000	9,120,000

- Highlight the Months from January to December
- In the "Alignment" group, under the "Home" tab, we have the three vertical alignments and the three horizontal alignments. For the vertical alignments, when we highlighted the months, it shows that the content of that range of cells is highlighted to the bottom.

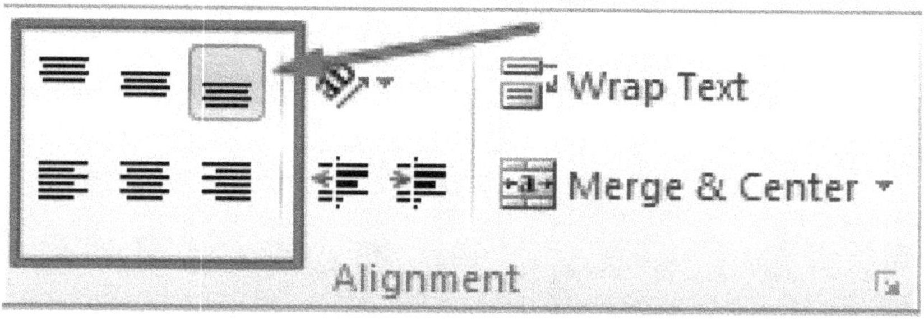

- If we want to align them to the middle, we click on the Middle alignment.

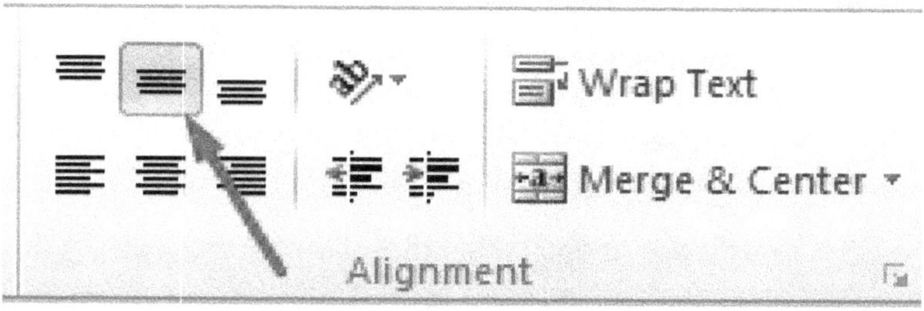

And the content of that row is moved to the middle with space at the top and bottom of each text as shown below.

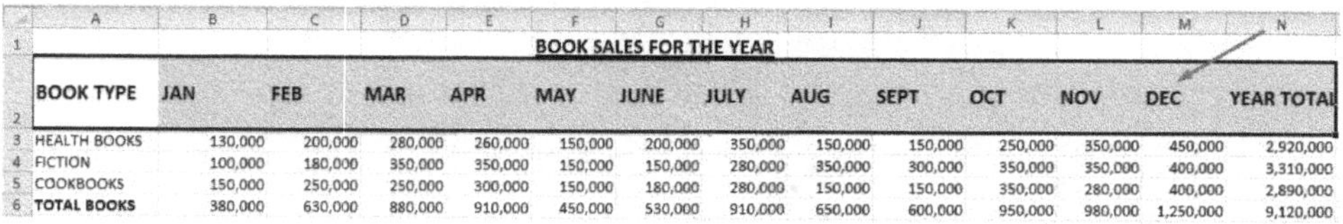

BOOK SALES FOR THE YEAR

BOOK TYPE	JAN	FEB	MAR	APR	MAY	JUNE	JULY	AUG	SEPT	OCT	NOV	DEC	YEAR TOTAL
HEALTH BOOKS	130,000	200,000	280,000	260,000	150,000	200,000	350,000	150,000	150,000	250,000	350,000	450,000	2,920,000
FICTION	100,000	180,000	350,000	350,000	150,000	150,000	280,000	350,000	300,000	350,000	350,000	400,000	3,310,000
COOKBOOKS	150,000	250,000	250,000	300,000	150,000	180,000	280,000	150,000	150,000	350,000	280,000	400,000	2,890,000
TOTAL BOOKS	380,000	630,000	880,000	910,000	450,000	530,000	910,000	650,000	600,000	950,000	980,000	1,250,000	9,120,000

- We align text to the top by clicking the top alignment.

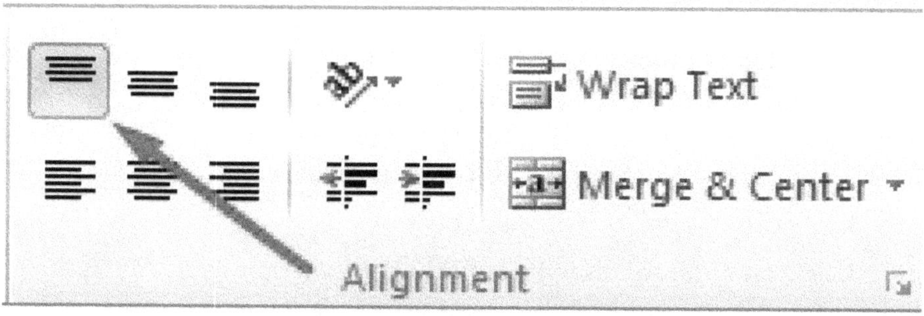

The top alignment moves the text to the top of the cell, leaving enough space beneath them in the highlighted cells.

BOOK TYPE	JAN	FEB	MAR	APR	MAY	JUNE	JULY	AUG	SEPT	OCT	NOV	DEC	YEAR TOTAL
HEALTH BOOKS	130,000	200,000	280,000	260,000	150,000	200,000	350,000	150,000	150,000	250,000	350,000	450,000	2,920,000
FICTION	100,000	180,000	350,000	350,000	150,000	150,000	280,000	350,000	300,000	350,000	350,000	400,000	3,310,000
COOKBOOKS	150,000	250,000	250,000	300,000	150,000	180,000	280,000	150,000	150,000	350,000	280,000	400,000	2,890,000
TOTAL BOOKS	380,000	630,000	880,000	910,000	450,000	530,000	910,000	650,000	600,000	950,000	980,000	1,250,000	9,120,000

- For Horizontal alignments, we can do left, center and right.

For orientation, you can change the orientation of text within a cell by clicking on the orientation menu within the alignment group.

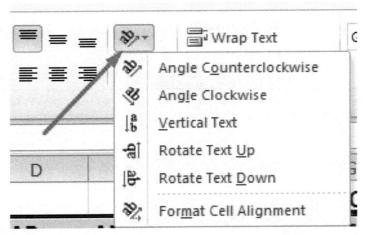

The orientation option rotates text within a cell to a diagonal angle or vertical orientation. To change the direction of a cell content;

- Highlight the cell or range of cells
- Click on 'orientation.'
- Select the orientation you want for the text e.g., vertical text, rotate text downward, etc.

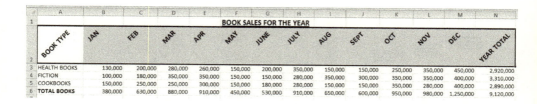

BOOK TYPE	JAN	FEB	MAR	APR	MAY	JUNE	JULY	AUG	SEPT	OCT	NOV	DEC	YEAR TOTAL
HEALTH BOOKS	130,000	200,000	280,000	260,000	150,000	200,000	350,000	150,000	150,000	250,000	350,000	450,000	2,920,000
FICTION	100,000	180,000	350,000	350,000	150,000	150,000	280,000	350,000	300,000	350,000	350,000	400,000	3,310,000
COOKBOOKS	150,000	250,000	250,000	300,000	150,000	180,000	280,000	150,000	150,000	350,000	280,000	400,000	2,890,000
TOTAL BOOKS	380,000	630,000	880,000	910,000	450,000	530,000	910,000	650,000	600,000	950,000	980,000	1,250,000	9,120,000

Text Wrapping

Text wrapping wraps text, which extends beyond the cell boundaries. If you type a text in a cell and it extends beyond the size of the cell, there are two ways you can format it. For instance, in our 'Book sales for the year' worksheet, the title 'Book Sales for the year transcends several cells (from F1 to H1). If we decide to type in anything in cell G1, it cuts off our title. We can fix this by either merging the cells that have the title or we perform a text wrap to keep the title within Cell F1. To merge the cells;

- We highlight the title 'Book Sales For The Year'
- Next, we go to the 'Home' Tab and under the 'Alignment' group, we select 'Merge & Center.' This merges the cells and places the text in the middle.

- Alternatively, we can wrap the text within a cell.
- Highlight the text
- Click on the 'Home' tab
- In the Alignment groups, select 'Wrap Text.'

- And it wraps the entire text to fit into a cell

	A	B	C	D	E	F	G	H	I	J
1						BOOK SALES FOR THE YEAR				
2	BOOK TYPE	JAN	FEB	MAR	APR	MAY	JUNE	JULY	AUG	SEPT
3	HEALTH BOOKS	130,000	200,000	280,000	260,000	150,000	200,000	350,000	150,000	150,000
4	FICTION	100,000	180,000	350,000	350,000	150,000	150,000	280,000	350,000	300,000
5	COOKBOOKS	150,000	250,000	250,000	300,000	150,000	180,000	280,000	150,000	150,000
6	TOTAL BOOKS	380,000	630,000	880,000	910,000	450,000	530,000	910,000	650,000	600,000
7										

Data Validation

Data Validation is a feature used in controlling what a user can enter into a cell. It simply displays a message to the user telling them what is allowed and what is not. Data Validation enables you to perform a number of actions like making lists of entries that restricts some values in a cell or range of cells. For instance, if we have a cell, we want to hold telephone numbers; we can use the Data Validation feature to prevent users from being able to input text. That way, we restrict the cell to numbers only, and we create a message which tells users what kind of data allowed in the cell and also creates a message that pops up when incorrect data is entered. Let's carry out an illustration to understand how data validation works. For instance, we have a form with the following columns - Name, Gender, Address, Telephone, and data of birth.

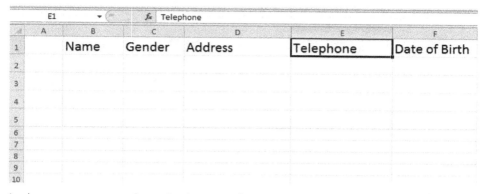

Let's say we want the telephone column to carry only whole numbers and no text, and the entire numbers should be precisely ten digits. We will select the telephone column

- Click on the 'Data' tab
- In the 'Data Tool' group, click on "Data Validation"

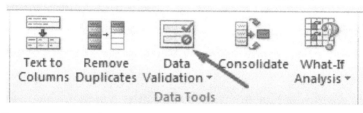

- This pop-open the Data Validation window

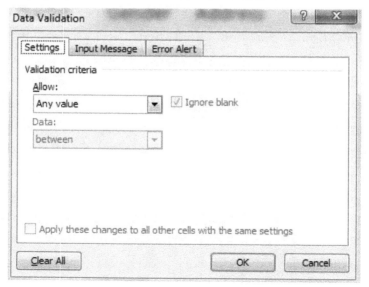

- On the Data Validation box, select "Allow" drop-down menu and select 'Whole Number.' Under "Data," select how the number should be. Should it be less than, greater than of exactly a particular number of digits? Since we prefer to use ten digits for the telephone column, we select 'equal to,' and the value is kept at ten.

- Next, click on 'Input Message' and type in the title and input message that should pop up when a cell within the telephone column is selected.

- Move to the Error Alert and key in the message that should pop-up as an alert if an invalid data is entered. Here you can select an alert icon that should pop-up as well and error message that should appear alongside.

- We can choose to make our gender column a list and make it 'Male' or 'Female.' Select 'List' from the "Allow" drop-down, next, type in the data that should be in the drop-down menu separated by a comma. Finally, enter input information and alert that should be displayed when a wrong item is selected.

- We could also use the "Allow" to set a range of numbers that the cell should carry. For instance, if we want a cell to carry numbers between 1 and 5, we will select 'Whole number' in the Allow drop-down menu and choose 'between' in the 'Data' section. Next, we input the Minimum number as one (1) and the Maximum number as five (5). Next, we will type in an 'input message' to allow users to know the number range they can input. For instance, "Please enter numbers between 1 and 5" any number above five (5) will not be accepted". Then we select 'Error Alert' that should pop-up plus the error message when a number outside the range chosen is inputted then click 'OK.' That way, only numbers between 1 and 5 can be inputted in that cell or range of cells, and any attempt to insert a number outside this range will bring up and Error Alert.

Let's look at another data validation illustration.

	A	B	C	D	E	F
1	Matriculation No	Name	Gender	Address	Telephone	Date of Birth
2						
3						
4						
5						
6						
7						
8						

We want students to input their information in the form above, starting with their matriculation number, and we want to ensure that no student enters a duplicate value in the Matriculation Number column because every student should have a unique matriculation number. We can set the matriculation No column not to accept duplicate information using Data Validation.

We need the **COUNTIF Function**, which is **=COUNTIF(range, criteria)** in this process. Here are the steps;

- Select the column you want duplications to be avoided
- Click on "Data Validation" in the 'Data' tab
- Under Data validation in the 'Settings' select 'Custom', and this will bring up the formula menu.

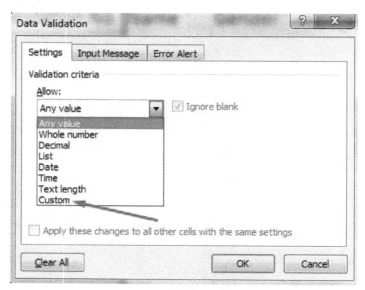

- Now, insert the **COUNTIF Function** in the Formula bar. What do we need for the **COUNTIF Function,** we need to identify if the range contains a duplicate. So we will select the Matriculation Number Column to identify if it contains duplicate. For our illustration, Matriculation No is in column A. So, we will check if the entire A column has a duplicate, starting from the first cell (A1). This is how we can translate the statement into **COUNTIF Function**

$$=COUNTIF(A:A,A1)<=1$$

This means we can enter a data into the selected column, but this data should not appear more than once. When it is zero (0), it means the data hasn't occurred yet, but when it is one (1), the data has occurred and cannot be repeated in another cell.

- Now enter the **COUNTIF Function** in the formula bar of the Data Validation dialogue box.

- Click 'OK'
- Now, if you enter any matriculation number twice, an error message will pop up. You can customize the error message.

What-if Tools

What-if Analysis helps users to try out different values for the formula in your sheet, using goal seek, data table and scenario manager. What-if analysis is a Data tool function. We will be looking at the three what-is functions one after the other. That is;

- Goal Seek
- Data Tables and
- Scenario Managers

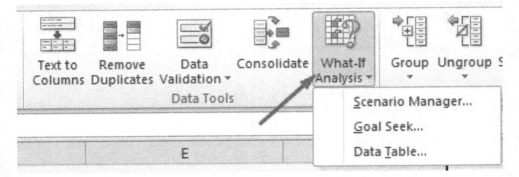

Now, let's look at how these three functions work.

Goal Seek Function

Goal seek is an inbuilt Excel tool that allows you to see how one data item in a formula impacts another. In other words, it helps users find the right input for the value they want. The Goal Seek function is used to answer a What-if type question because you can adjust one cell entry to see the result. This tool is mostly used in finance, sales, and forecasting scenarios. Let's illustrate Goal Seek function using the data below.

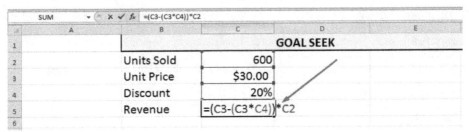

The above model contains the following information, Unit sold – 600, Until price - $30, Discount on each sale – 20%, and the Revenue - $14,400.00. The Revenue is derived from the formula =(C3-(C3*C4))*C2.

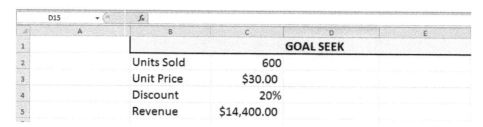

	A	B	C	D	E
1				GOAL SEEK	
2		Units Sold	600		
3		Unit Price	$30.00		
4		Discount	20%		
5		Revenue	$14,400.00		

Now, using 'Goal Seek' function, we need to identify how many units have to be sold to reach a $20,000 revenue goal while keeping the unit price and discount the same. To get this done, we click on "Goal Seek" in the Data tab. In the Goal Seek dialogue box, there are three values we need to enter – the 'set cell,' 'to value,' and 'by changing cell.'

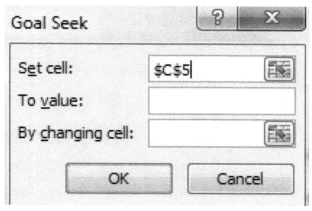

The set cell is the cell you wish to increase. In our illustration, the set cell is cell C5. The 'To Value' is what value you need in the cell or you intend to achieve. In our case, it is $20,000.00. So we type in 20000. Finally, the "By changing Cell," this is the cell that holds the number of units we need to sell to achieve $20,000.00 in revenue. So we select cell C2 as our "By Changing Cell" address.

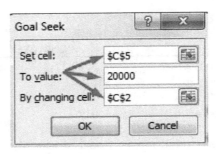

Click on "OK," and it will automatically calculate the number of units we need to sell to attain our $20,000.00 goal.

From the calculation, we need to sell 834 units to attain a revenue of $20,000.

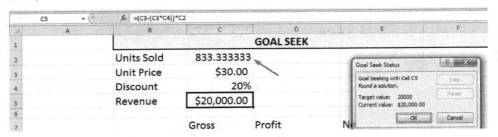

Next, we have sales figures for Spring, Winter and Summer, and we want to use these data to find out how much sales we could make in Fall to have a Net Profit Goal of $50,000.00 using goal seek function.

	C	D	E
1		GOAL SEEK	
2	833.333333		
3	$30.00		
4	20%		
5	$20,000.00		
6			
7	Gross	Profit	Net
8	$100,000.00	10%	$10,000.00
9	$150,000.00	15%	$22,500.00
10	$50,000.00	12%	$6,000.00
11		15%	0
12	**Net Profit Goal**		$38,500.00

Now, with Goal Seek, we have to find out what the gross sales for Fall is and we will take 15% of that value as our Net Profit for Fall and when the Net Profit for Spring, Winter, Summer and Fall are added, we should have a Total Net Profit of $50,000.00. To get 15% of the Gross sales for Fall, we enter the formula in such a way that we get 10% of the content of C11 in Cell E11. We type in

$$=C11*15/100$$

Or better put

$$=C11*D11$$

Then in the 'Goal Seek' dialogue box, we input our current Net profit ($38,500.00) which is housed in Cell E12 into our 'Set Sell,' Next, we input our target value which is $50,000.00 in the 'To Value' box and the Gross Sales for Fall which is the unknown (Cell C11) is placed in the 'By Changing Cells' box.

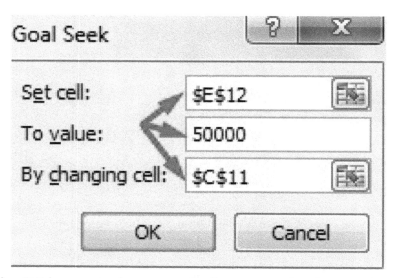

Click the OK button, and it automatically gives us the Gross Sales for Fall that we should get if we are to have a total Net Sales of $50,000.00.

	A	B	C	D	E	F
1				GOAL SEEK		
2		Units Sold	833.333333			
3		Unit Price	$30.00			
4		Discount	20%			
5		Revenue	$20,000.00			
6						
7			Gross	Profit	Net	
8		Spring Sales	$100,000.00		10%	$10,000.00
9		Winter Sales	$150,000.00		15%	$22,500.00
10		Summer Sales	$50,000.00		12%	$6,000.00
11		Fall Sales	$76,666.67		15%	11500.0005
12			**Net Profit Goal**			$50,000.00
13						

From our Goal Seek Function application, we need a Gross Sales of $76,666.67 and a Net Sales of $11500,00 for Fall to get a total Net Sales of $50,000.00

Data Tables

The data table is one of Excel's What-if analysis features. It seeks the result of multiple inputs at the same time. Let's look at how Data Tables work using the sheet below;

	A	B	C	D	E	F	G
1				DATA TABLES			
2		Sales Price	1800				
3		Quantity	25				
4		Cost Price	1500				
5		Discount on Sales	10%				
6			Total Revenue	40500			
7							
8			10%				
9			15%				
10			20%				
11			25%				
12			30%				
13			35%				
14			40%				
15							

In In the above sheet, we have a sales price, quantity sold, cost price, a discount on sales, which is 10%, and Total Revenue, which is 40,500. Now, we will find the total revenue when the discount percentage is changed. Note that we got the total revenue using the function below.'

$$=(C2-(C2*C5))*C3$$

Find 10% of 1800, which is 180, then subtract the result from 1800 (1800 - 180 = 1620) then multiply the result by the quantity (25). That is 1620 x 25 = 40,500.

	A	B	C	D	E	F	G
	SUM		× ✓ fx =(C2-(C2*C5))*C3				
1				DATA TABLES			
2		Sales Price	1800				
3		Quantity	25				
4		Cost Price	1500				
5		Discount on Sales	10%				
6			Total Revenue =(C2-(C2*C5))*C3				
7							
8			10%				
9			15%				
10			20%				
11			25%				
12			30%				
13			35%				
14			40%				
15							

So after 10% discount on sales, we have 40,500. Now we need to look for the total revenue at 15%, 20%, 25%, 30%, 35% and 40%. Instead of doing it one after the other, we will use the What-if Function. To do this, let's follow the steps below;

- Select the data where we need the results

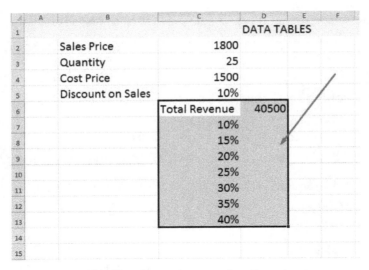

	A	B	C	D	E	F
1				DATA TABLES		
2		Sales Price	1800			
3		Quantity	25			
4		Cost Price	1500			
5		Discount on Sales	10%			
6			Total Revenue	40500		
7			10%			
8			15%			
9			20%			
10			25%			
11			30%			
12			35%			
13			40%			
14						
15						

- Click on the "What-if Analysis in the 'Data' tab

- Select the 'Data Table' option

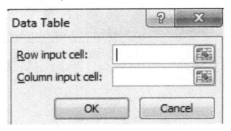

- On the Data Table dialogue box, we have the option to select between "Row input cell" or "Column input Cell." Our data will be coming in the column, so we will select the column input cell and click on the cell holding the first percentage (10%) from the base data, which is in our case Cell C5. (10%) from the base data which is in our case Cell C5.

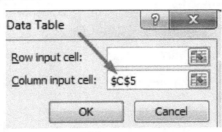

- Click "OK" and we get the percentage for the other percentage.

	C6	▾	f_x Total Revenue			
	A	B	C	D	E	F
1				DATA TABLES		
2		Sales Price	1800			
3		Quantity	25			
4		Cost Price	1500			
5		Discount on Sales	10%			
6			Total Revenue	40500		
7			10%	40500		
8			15%	38250		
9			20%	36000		
10			25%	33750		
11			30%	31500		
12			35%	29250		
13			40%	27000		
14						
15						

In our second example, we will look at an instance where we need to find the total profit if the discount percentage and sales price changes as shown below;

	N16	▾	f_x								
	A	B	C	D	E	F	G	H	I	J	K	L
1				DATA TABLES							
2		Sales Price	1800								
3		Quantity	25								
4		Cost Price	1500								
5		Discount or	10%								
6			Total Revenue	40500							
7											
8		Total Profit	3000	1800	2000	2500	3000	3500	4000	4500	5000
9			10%								
10			15%								
11			20%								
12			25%								
13			30%								
14			35%								
15			40%								
16											

Our total profit is 3000, when we have a sales price of 1800, sold 25 units and have a cost price of 1500 and a discount of 10%. We got this Total profit using the formula =((C2-(C2*C5))-C4)*C3.

185

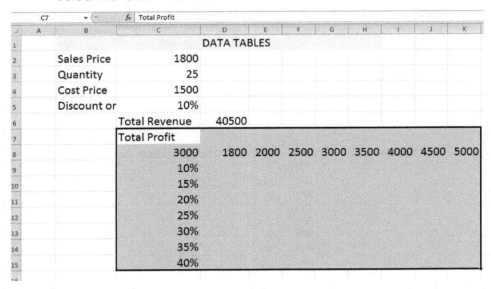

Now let's see what happens when we change our discount and sales price.

Now, here are the steps to find out the change in values using Data tables;

- Select the data where we need the results

- Click on What-if analysis and select Data Tables

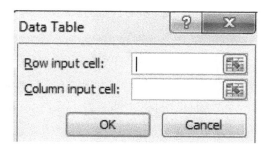

- In In this illustration, we have both rows and column input cells. The Row input cell is our sales price, which Cell C2, while our Column input cell is our first discount in the base data (10%) housed in Cell C5.

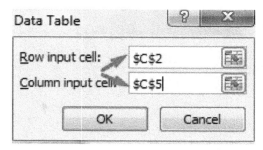

- Click OK

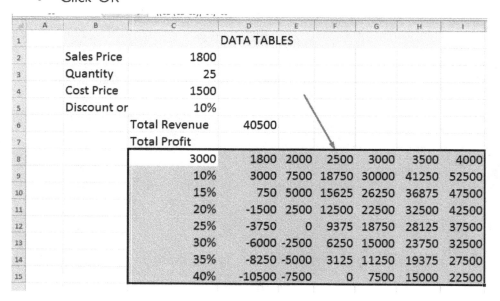

	A	B	C	D	E	F	G	H	I
1			DATA TABLES						
2		Sales Price	1800						
3		Quantity	25						
4		Cost Price	1500						
5		Discount or	10%						
6			Total Revenue	40500					
7			Total Profit						
8			3000	1800	2000	2500	3000	3500	4000
9			10%	3000	7500	18750	30000	41250	52500
10			15%	750	5000	15625	26250	36875	47500
11			20%	-1500	2500	12500	22500	32500	42500
12			25%	-3750	0	9375	18750	28125	37500
13			30%	-6000	-2500	6250	15000	23750	32500
14			35%	-8250	-5000	3125	11250	19375	27500
15			40%	-10500	-7500	0	7500	15000	22500

Scenario Managers

Scenario manager in Excel creates different groups of values or scenarios and switches between them. Let's assume you own a book store and have 100 books in stock. You sell a certain percentage for the highest price of $60 and a certain percentage for the lower-priced book of $30.

	A	B	C	D
1				
2		Total No of Books	percentage of highest price	
3		100	70%	
4				
5		No. of Books	Unit Profit	
6	Highest price	70	$60	
7	Lowest Price	30	$30	
8		Total Profit	5100	
9				

We will insert a formula in our list. For Cell B2 to get the 70% No. of books sold thus total books multiply by the highest price which is 70%.

$$=B3*C3$$

	A	B	C	D
1				
2		Total No of Books	percentage of highest price	
3		100	70%	
4				
5		No. of Books	Unit Profit	
6	Highest price	=B3*C3	$60	
7	Lowest Price	30	$30	
8		Total Profit	5100	
9				
10				

While that of B7 is given as total books sold minus the highest-priced book

$$=B3-B6$$

	A	B	C	D
1				
2		Total No of Books	percentage of highest price	
3		100	70%	
4				
5		No. of Books	Unit Profit	
6	Highest price	70	$60	
7	Lowest Price	=B3-B6	$30	
8		Total Profit	5100	
9				

We also insert a formula for the total profit thus

$$=(B6*C6)+(B7*C7)$$

	A	B	C	D
1				
2		Total No of Books	percentage of highest price	
3		100	70%	
4				
5		No. of Books	Unit Profit	
6	Highest price	70	$60	
7	Lowest Price	30	$30	
8		Total Profit	=(B6*C6)+(B7*C7)	
9				

Now, let's say we want to increase the percentage of the highest price books to 80% and 90%, what will it look like? Or what profit we will get. We can use Scenario Manager to do this. Here are the steps;

- Click on What-if analysis and select Scenario manager
- In the pop-up scenario manager window, there is an option to 'Add' the scenario.
- Click on the Add option on the scenario manager dialogue box to add scenario options. The options include scenario name, changing cells, and comments. Our Scenario name is "70% increase" you can use any name for this.

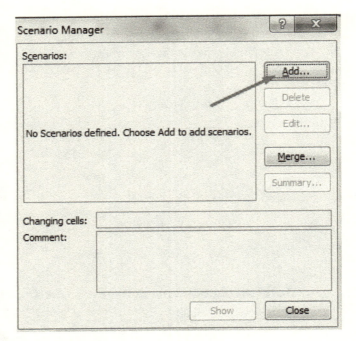

- Put anything in the scenario name
- 'Changing Cells' refers to the information we wish to change. For our illustration, it is the percentage of the books sold at the highest price i.e., the cell address holding 70% (Cell C3).

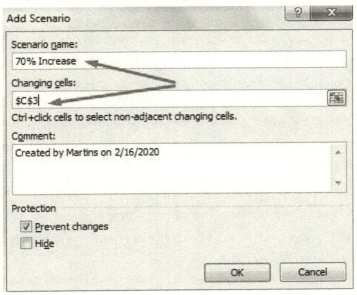

- And click OK.
- Once you click on the OK button, you get a Scenario Value dialogue box saying, "Enter value for each of the changing cells." The value that needs to change is 70%, which is 0.7. This is derived from 70 divides by 100 equal to 0.7.

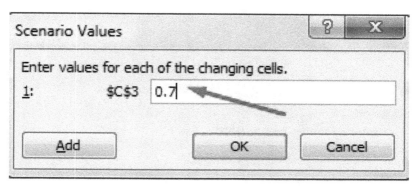

- Click on "OK"
- Now, you will notice that the first scenario manager information has been added (which we named 70% increase).

- Next, let's add the data for 80%. Click on the 'Add' button
- Name this new scenario 80% increase and the changing cells, remain Cell C3, then click OK.

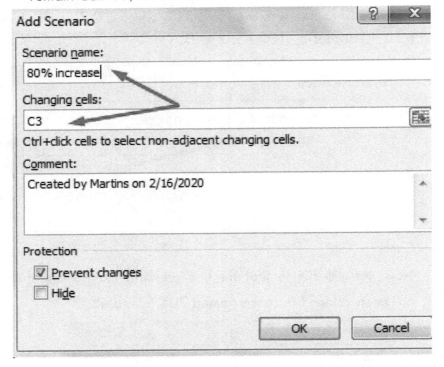

- Next, change the "Enter values for each of the changing cells" to 0.8. I.e., 80%, which also is equal to 80 divided by 100.

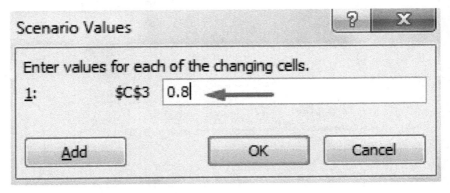

- Click OK

- We have added two scenarios to the scenario manager (70% and 80% increase). Now let's add the third scenario, "90% increase."
- Click on the 'Add' button to add the third scenario of a 90% increase. We name the third scenario 90% increase, and the 'Changing Cells' remains the same at C3

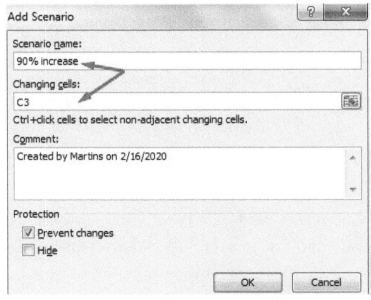

- Click 'OK'
- Change the 'Enter Values for each of the changing cells" to 0.9.

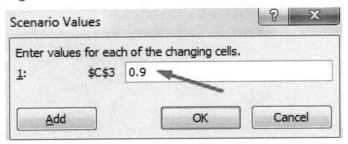

- Click 'OK' to add the 90% increase scenario to the scenario manager

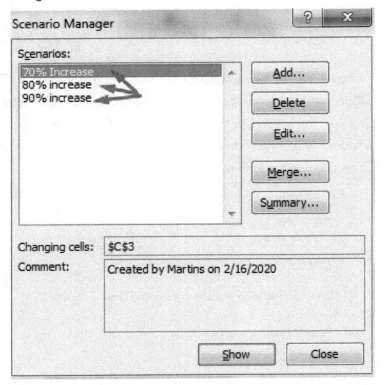

Now that we have the three scenarios, we can see the result for a 70% increase, an 80% increase, and a 90% increase by simply click on the percentage value we want to see and click on the "Show" button.

Below is the result when we click on a 70% increase and click on the "Show" button.

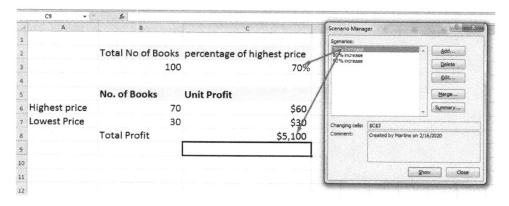

We could see the total profit was $5100.

Next, we select 80% increase and click on "show."

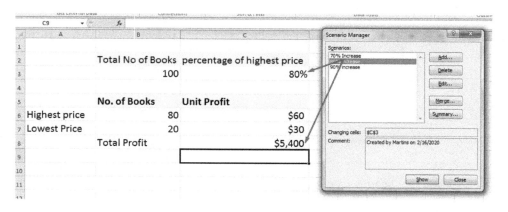

Our Total profit changes to $5400. Finally, when we selected 90% increase, and click on "Show", we get $5700.

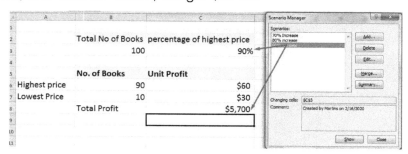

Finally, if we click on "Summary" on the Scenario Manager Dialogue box,

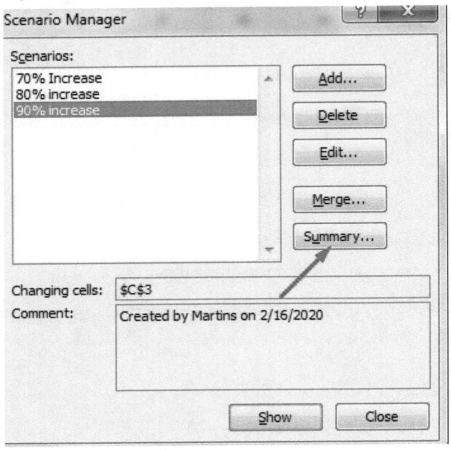

It gives you an option to produce either a scenario summary or a scenario pivot table report.

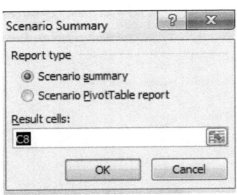

This opens a new Excel sheet where the results of all percentages stored in the scenario manager as shown below;

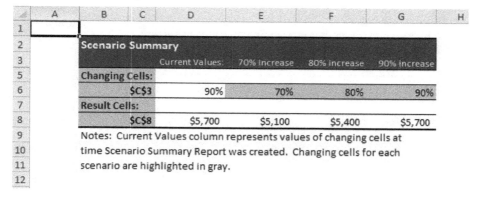

	A	B	C	D	E	F	G	H
1								
2		Scenario Summary						
3				Current Values:	70% increase	80% increase	90% increase	
5		Changing Cells:						
6			C3	90%	70%	80%	90%	
7		Result Cells:						
8			C8	$5,700	$5,100	$5,400	$5,700	
9		Notes: Current Values column represents values of changing cells at						
10		time Scenario Summary Report was created. Changing cells for each						
11		scenario are highlighted in gray.						
12								

Remove Duplicates

Text to Columns   Remove Duplicates   Data Validation ▾   Consolidate   What-If Analysis ▾

Data Tools

Duplicate text or data can be removed using the Remove Duplicate function. This is also a data tool option. We can remove duplicate in a datasheet by highlighting the range of cells where the duplicates is, and then click on the 'Data' tab and select "Remove Duplicate."

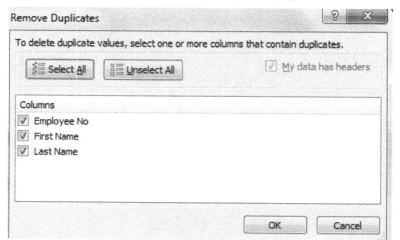

197

Duplicate text or data can be removed using the Remove Duplicate function. This is also a data tool option. We can remove duplicate in a datasheet by highlighting the range of cells where the duplicates are, and then click on the 'Data' tab and select "Remove Duplicate."

Data Sorting

The sort function is a data sanitization function. We can use the sort function to arrange data in a worksheet in alphabetical order. It could be in increasing or decreasing alphabetical order. Another way to sort data in numerical order is by their column items.

Filter Option

The filter option enables filters to be applied to a selected cell. Once the filter is activated, arrows pop-up on each of the column headers. You can choose a filter for the column by click on the arrow where you could sort the selected column alphabetically or by colors. Custom filter works when you click on any of the data drop-downs, and in the drop-down, you will see the 'Text' filter, and under the text filter, you have the custom filter.

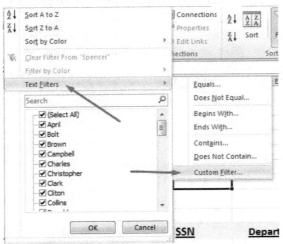

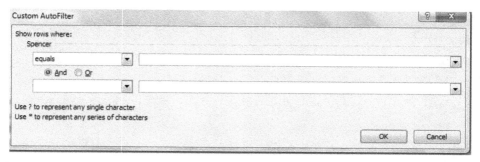

Custom Filter will work when you have numerical data where you can use similar to equals. It is greater than, does not equal, is greater than or equal to, is less than, ends with, contains, etc.

Employee No	First Name	Last Name	SSN	Department	Employment Date	Hour	Rate	Gross
				Midas Concept LLC				
				Payroll				
b2437110	Mark	Spencer	450012432	Admin	1/22/2019	50	$75.00	$3,000.00
b2437111	John	Bolt	341112434	Sales	7/24/2019	50	$44.30	$1,772.00
a2437112	James	Phrase	670022435	Sales	2/24/2018	52	$19.90	$835.00
b2437113	Luther	Miles	882012539	Marketing	6/3/2017	58	$15.00	$1,770.00
2437114	Harry	Cliton	553112632	Sales	12/28/2019	58	$55.50	$1,623.00
2437115	Bells	Simpson	125512442	Personnel	1/5/2017	45	$12.00	$430.00
b2437116	Bob	Kelly	522001248	Human Resource	8/23/2019	45	$12.00	$430.00
b2437117	Martins	April	538012498	Sales	8/13/2018	58	$15.50	$1,807.00
2437118	James	Kingsley	587012489	Admin	9/27/2018	58	$49.00	$1,960.00
2437119	Robert	Hume	480026440	Sales	10/7/2019	30	$55.95	$1,808.00
b2437120	Harold	Jason	552812450	Sales	8/30/2019	30	$45.20	$1,920
b2437121	David	Kessington	421596508	Sales	2/11/2019	25	$33.16	$1,025.85
b2437122	Davis	Gray	207843531	Marketing	3/27/2017	30	$32.64	$1,012.66
a2437123	Benjamin	Samuel	317960683	Marketing	5/7/2018	25	$32.12	$999.47
b2437124	Anderson	Smith	527728054	Sales	2/21/2018	45	$31.59	$986.28
a2437125	Wright	Clark	200968363	Director	7/17/2017	29	$31.07	$973.09

For instance, if we want to filter employees names based on their salary information, i.e., those who are earning less than $1000 and those making more than $1500

We select the Entire columns in the worksheet > click on Data > select "Filters." Now we click on the drop-down arrow by the Gross Column header > select "Number Filters" > "Less than" 1000 and "is greater than" 1500. Hit the Enter Key.

Only the employee details that earn less than $1000 and greater than $1500 will be displayed on the list.

Insert Comment

You can insert a comment on a cell so that when the cursor is hovered over the cell, the comment is displayed. To insert a comment in a cell, select the cell or range of cells > right click on the mouse and select "Insert Comment."

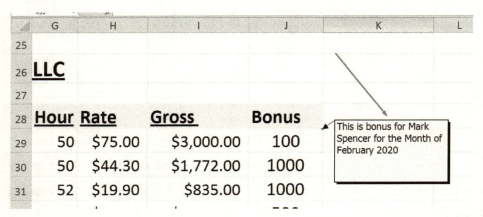

You can remove the cell by selecting the cell > right click and select "Delete Comment."

Average

The **Average Function** returns the average (arithmetic mean) of the arguments. It has a general syntax thus

$$=\text{Average(Cell Address1, Cell Address2, Cell Address3,...)}$$

Or

$$=\text{Average(cell Array1, Cell Array2,...)}$$

Let's say we need to verify the average salaries paid to the employees in Midas Concept LLC.

	A	B	C	D	E	F	G	H	I	J	K
						Midas Concept LLC					
						Payroll					
28	Employee No	First Name	Last Name	SSN	Department	Employment Date	Hour	Rate	Gross		Average
29	b2437110	Mark	Spencer	450012432	Admin	1/22/2019	50	$75.00	$3,000.00		
30	b2437111	John	Bolt	341112434	Sales	7/24/2019	50	$44.30	$1,772.00		
31	a2437112	James	Phrase	670022435	Sales	2/24/2018	52	$19.90	$835.00		
32	b2437113	Luther	Miles	882012539	Marketing	6/3/2017	58	$15.00	$1,770.00		
33	2437114	Harry	Cliton	553112632	Sales	12/28/2019	58	$55.50	$1,623.00		
34	2437115	Bells	Simpson	125512442	Personnel	1/5/2017	45	$12.00	$430.00		
35	b2437116	Bob	Kelly	522001248	Human Resource	8/23/2019	45	$12.00	$430.00		
36	b2437117	Martins	April	538012498	Sales	8/13/2018	58	$15.50	$1,807.00		
37	2437118	James	Kingsley	587012489	Admin	9/27/2018	58	$49.00	$1,960.00		
38	2437119	Robert	Hume	480026440	Sales	10/7/2019	30	$55.95	$1,808.00		
39	b2437120	Harold	Jason	552812450	Sales	8/30/2019	30	$45.20	$1,920		
40	b2437121	David	Kessington	421596508	Sales	2/11/2019	25	$33.16	$1,025.85		
41	b2437122	Davis	Gray	207843531	Marketing	3/27/2017	30	$32.64	$1,012.66		
42	a2437123	Benjamin	Samuel	317960683	Marketing	5/7/2018	25	$32.12	$999.47		
43	b2437124	Anderson	Smith	527728054	Sales	2/21/2018	45	$31.59	$986.28		
44	a2437125	Wright	Clark	200968363	Director	7/17/2017	29	$31.07	$973.09		
45	a2437126	Mitchell	Johnson	523191905	Procurement	5/14/2017	32	$30.54	$959.90		
46	a2437127	Thomas	Rodriguez	213597710	Sales	11/24/2016	45	$30.02	$946.71		
47	a2437128	Jackson	Perez	519214366	Marketing	12/9/2017	56	$29.50	$1,867.00		
48	a2437129	Lewis	Hill	337946786	Finance	3/24/2019	40	$28.97	$1,270.00		
49	a2437130	Robert	Jones	200824449	Sales	4/3/2016	35	$28.45	$907.14		

The salaries for Midas Employees is on column **I**, so we input the function,

=AVERAGE(I:I)

When we hit the ENTER Key, it returns the average salaries of all employees as 1161.990

Median Function

The **Median Function** is a statistical function that returns the median of a given number. The median is the middle number in the set of numbers. For instance, if we have 10,12,15, the median function will return 12 as the middle number.

	J	K	L	M	N
2					
3		**Median**			
4					
5		=MEDIAN(L5,M5,N5)	10	12	15
6					
7					

When we hit the ENTER key, it returns 12.

	J	K	L	M	N
2					
3		**Median**			
4					
5		12	10	12	15
6					

Likewise, we can find the Median Salary in our Midas Concept LLC payroll using the median function

=MEDIAN(I:I)

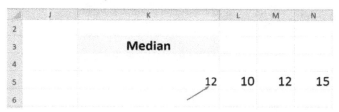

When we hit ENTER, we get the middle value of the Salary column, which is $835.

Employee No	First Name	Last Name	SSN	Department	Employment Date	Hour	Rate	Gross		Median
										Midas Concept LLC
										Payroll
b2437110	Mark	Spencer	450012432	Admin	1/22/2019	50	$75.00	$3,000.00		835
b2437111	John	Bolt	341112434	Sales	7/24/2019	50	$44.30	$1,772.00		
a2437112	James	Phrase	670022435	Sales	2/24/2018	52	$19.90	$835.00		
b2437113	Luther	Miles	882012539	Marketing	6/3/2017	58	$15.00	$1,770.00		
2437114	Harry	Cliton	553112632	Sales	12/28/2019	58	$55.50	$1,623.00		
2437115	Bells	Simpson	125512442	Personnel	1/5/2017	45	$12.00	$430.00		
b2437116	Bob	Kelly	522001248	Human Resource	8/23/2019	45	$12.00	$430.00		
b2437117	Martins	April	538012498	Sales	8/13/2018	58	$15.50	$1,807.00		
2437118	James	Kingsley	587012489	Admin	9/27/2018	58	$49.00	$1,960.00		
2437119	Robert	Hume	480026440	Sales	10/7/2019	30	$55.95	$1,808.00		
b2437120	Harold	Jason	552812450	Sales	8/30/2019	30	$45.20	$1,920		
b2437121	David	Kessington	421596508	Sales	2/11/2019	25	$33.16	$1,025.85		
b2437122	Davis	Gray	207843531	Marketing	3/27/2017	30	$32.64	$1,012.66		
a2437123	Benjamin	Samuel	317960683	Marketing	5/7/2018	25	$32.12	$999.47		
b2437124	Anderson	Smith	527728054	Sales	2/21/2018	45	$31.59	$986.28		
a2437125	Wright	Clark	200968363	Director	7/17/2017	29	$31.07	$973.09		
a2437126	Mitchell	Johnson	523191905	Procurement	5/14/2017	32	$30.54	$959.90		
a2437127	Thomas	Rodriguez	213597710	Sales	11/24/2016	45	$30.02	$946.71		
a2437128	Jackson	Perez	519214366	Marketing	12/9/2017	56	$29.50	$1,867.00		
a2437129	Lewis	Hill	337946786	Finance	3/24/2019	40	$28.97	$1,270.00		
a2437130	Robert	Jones	200824449	Sales	4/3/2016	35	$28.45	$907.14		

Mode Function

The Excel Mode Function returns the most frequently occurring numbers in a numeric data set. This function only works with numbers. It will identify the amount of the number that occurs maximum time in the range of cells. To illustrate with our Midas Concept LLC payroll, we input the formula;

$$=MODE(I:I)$$

SUM								=MODE.MULT(I:I)		
Employee No	First Name	Last Name	SSN	Department	Employment Date	Hour	Rate	Gross		Mode
										Midas Concept LLC
										Payroll
b2437110	Mark	Spencer	450012432	Admin	1/22/2019	50	$75.00	$3,000.00		=MODE.MULT(I:I)
b2437111	John	Bolt	341112434	Sales	7/24/2019	50	$44.30	$1,772.00		
a2437112	James	Phrase	670022435	Sales	2/24/2018	52	$19.90	$835.00		
b2437113	Luther	Miles	882012539	Marketing	6/3/2017	58	$15.00	$1,770.00		
2437114	Harry	Cliton	553112632	Sales	12/28/2019	58	$55.50	$1,623.00		
2437115	Bells	Simpson	125512442	Personnel	1/5/2017	45	$12.00	$430.00		
b2437116	Bob	Kelly	522001248	Human Resource	8/23/2019	45	$12.00	$430.00		
b2437117	Martins	April	538012498	Sales	8/13/2018	58	$15.50	$1,807.00		
2437118	James	Kingsley	587012489	Admin	9/27/2018	58	$49.00	$1,960.00		
2437119	Robert	Hume	480026440	Sales	10/7/2019	30	$55.95	$1,808.00		
b2437120	Harold	Jason	552812450	Sales	8/30/2019	30	$45.20	$1,920		
b2437121	David	Kessington	421596508	Sales	2/11/2019	25	$33.16	$1,025.85		
b2437122	Davis	Gray	207843531	Marketing	3/27/2017	30	$32.64	$1,012.66		
a2437123	Benjamin	Samuel	317960683	Marketing	5/7/2018	25	$32.12	$999.47		
b2437124	Anderson	Smith	527728054	Sales	2/21/2018	45	$31.59	$986.28		
a2437125	Wright	Clark	200968363	Director	7/17/2017	29	$31.07	$973.09		
a2437126	Mitchell	Johnson	523191905	Procurement	5/14/2017	32	$30.54	$959.90		
a2437127	Thomas	Rodriguez	213597710	Sales	11/24/2016	45	$30.02	$946.71		
a2437128	Jackson	Perez	519214366	Marketing	12/9/2017	56	$29.50	$1,867.00		
a2437129	Lewis	Hill	337946786	Finance	3/24/2019	40	$28.97	$1,270.00		
a2437130	Robert	Jones	200824449	Sales	4/3/2016	35	$28.45	$907.14		

When we hit ENTER, we get $430 as the most occurred salary on our payroll.

Standard Deviation Function

The Excel Standard deviation function calculates the standard deviation in a sample set of data. It is a measure of how much variant there is in a set of numbers compared to the average of the numbers. The standard deviation dot S (STDEV.S) function is meant to estimate standard deviation on a sample and ignores logical values and text in the sample. If the data represents an entire population, we use the Standard Deviation dot (STDEV.P) Function.

For instance, a sample of a few students and their scores in a subject where picked as shown below;

	L	M	N	O	P	Q
1						
2			**Number**	**Score**		**Standard Deviation**
3			1	102		
4			2	99		
5			3	97		
6			4	100		
7			5	98		
8			6	105		
9			7	102		
10			8	105		
11			9	89		
12						
13						
14						

So we only picked a sample and not using the entire student data. Since we are using a sampling technique in the above example, we use the STDEV.S Function. We give the formula thus;

=STDEV.S(O3:O11)

SUM			▼ × ✓ *fx*	=STDEV.S(O3:O11)

	L	M	N	O		Q
1						
2			**Number**	**Score**		**Standard Deviation**
3			1	102		=STDEV.S(O3:O11)
4			2	99		
5			3	97		
6			4	100		
7			5	98		
8			6	105		
9			7	102		
10			8	105		
11			9	89		

When you press ENTER, we have the value as 4.89

	L	M	N	O	P	Q
1						
2			**Number**	**Score**		**Standard Deviation**
3			1	102		4.898979486
4			2	99		
5			3	97		
6			4	100		
7			5	98		
8			6	105		
9			7	102		
10			8	105		
11			9	89		

If you have a full population, let us say you have all the marks of all the students in the school you will need to use STDEV.P to calculate the Standard Deviation.

Large Function

The Excel Large Function returns the Kth largest value from the sample. The general syntax for the Large function is given thus;

=LARGE(Cell Array, K)

For example, if we go back to our Midas Concept Payroll data on the employee salary list, we can identify the largest salary been paid to employees. We can do this with the aid of the Large function.

=LARGE(I:I,1)

K means the 1,2,3,4,5,...n number of salaries paid. For instance, if we want to know the first highest paid salary, we input k as 1, but if we intend to identify the second highest salary been paid, k becomes 2, the third-highest, K becomes 3 and so on.

Now, let's look at the overall highest salary paid to an employee.

=LARGE(I:I,1)

	SUM					=LARGE(I:I,1)					
	A	B	C	D	E	F	G	H	I	J	K
1						**Midas Concept LLC**					
2						Payroll					
3	Employee No	First Name	Last Name	SSN	Department	Employment Date	Hour	Rate	Gross		Large
4	b2437110	Mark	Spencer	450012432	Admin	1/22/2019	50	$75.00	$3,000.00		=LARGE(I:I,1)
5	b2437111	John	Bolt	341112434	Sales	7/24/2019	50	$44.30	$1,772.00		
6	a2437112	James	Phrase	670022435	Sales	2/24/2018	52	$19.90	$835.00		
7	b2437113	Luther	Miles	882012539	Marketing	6/3/2017	58	$15.00	$1,770.00		
8	2437114	Harry	Cliton	553112632	Sales	12/28/2019	58	$55.50	$1,623.00		
9	2437115	Bells	Simpson	125512442	Personnel	1/5/2017	45	$12.00	$430.00		
10	b2437116	Bob	Kelly	522001248	Human Resource	8/23/2019	45	$12.00	$430.00		
11	b2437117	Martins	April	538012498	Sales	8/13/2018	58	$15.50	$1,807.00		
12	2437118	James	Kingsley	587012489	Admin	9/27/2018	58	$49.00	$1,960.00		
13	2437119	Robert	Hume	480026440	Sales	10/7/2019	30	$55.95	$1,808.00		
14	b2437120	Harold	Jason	552812450	Sales	8/30/2019	30	$45.20	$1,920		
15	b2437121	David	Kessington	421596508	Sales	2/11/2019	25	$33.16	$1,025.85		
16	b2437122	Davis	Gray	207843531	Marketing	3/27/2017	30	$32.64	$1,012.66		
17	a2437123	Benjamin	Samuel	317960683	Marketing	5/7/2018	25	$32.12	$999.47		
18	b2437124	Anderson	Smith	527728054	Sales	2/21/2018	45	$31.59	$986.28		
19	a2437125	Wright	Clark	200968363	Director	7/17/2017	29	$31.07	$973.09		
20	a2437126	Mitchell	Johnson	523191905	Procurement	5/14/2017	32	$30.54	$959.90		
21	a2437127	Thomas	Rodriguez	213597710	Sales	11/24/2016	45	$30.02	$946.71		
22	a2437128	Jackson	Perez	519214366	Marketing	12/9/2017	56	$29.50	$1,867.00		

When we hit ENTER, we got $9562.00 as the highest salary paid to an employee in Midas Concept LLC.

	A	B	C	D	E	F	G	H	I	J	K
1						Midas Concept LLC					
2						Payroll					
3	Employee No	First Name	Last Name	SSN	Department	Employment Date	Hour	Rate	Gross		Large
4	b2437110	Mark	Spencer	450012432	Admin	1/22/2019	50	$75.00	$3,000.00		9562
5	b2437111	John	Bolt	341112434	Sales	7/24/2019	50	$44.30	$1,772.00		
6	a2437112	James	Phrase	670022435	Sales	2/24/2018	52	$19.90	$835.00		
7	b2437113	Luther	Miles	882012539	Marketing	6/3/2017	58	$15.00	$1,770.00		
8	2437114	Harry	Cliton	553112632	Sales	12/28/2019	58	$55.50	$1,623.00		
9	2437115	Bells	Simpson	125512442	Personnel	1/5/2017	45	$12.00	$430.00		
10	b2437116	Bob	Kelly	522001248	Human Resource	8/23/2019	45	$12.00	$430.00		
11	b2437117	Martins	April	538012498	Sales	8/13/2018	58	$15.50	$1,807.00		
12	2437118	James	Kingsley	587012489	Admin	9/27/2018	58	$49.00	$1,960.00		
13	2437119	Robert	Hume	480026440	Sales	10/7/2019	30	$55.95	$1,808.00		
14	b2437120	Harold	Jason	552812450	Sales	8/30/2019	30	$45.20	$1,920		
15	b2437121	David	Kessington	421596508	Sales	2/11/2019	25	$33.16	$1,025.85		
16	b2437122	Davis	Gray	207843531	Marketing	3/27/2017	30	$32.64	$1,012.66		
17	a2437123	Benjamin	Samuel	317960683	Marketing	5/7/2018	25	$32.12	$999.47		
18	b2437124	Anderson	Smith	527728054	Sales	2/21/2018	45	$31.59	$986.28		
19	a2437125	Wright	Clark	200968363	Director	7/17/2017	29	$31.07	$973.09		
20	a2437126	Mitchell	Johnson	523191905	Procurement	5/14/2017	32	$30.54	$959.90		
21	a2437127	Thomas	Rodriguez	213597710	Sales	11/24/2016	45	$30.02	$946.71		
22	a2437128	Jackson	Perez	519214366	Marketing	12/9/2017	56	$29.50	$1,867.00		

Now let's find out the second-highest-paid salary amount. We use the function

$$=LARGE(I:I,2)$$

	A	B	C	D	E	F	G	H	I	J	K
	SUM				X ✓ fx	=LARGE(I:I,2)					
1						Midas Concept LLC					
2						Payroll					
3	Employee No	First Name	Last Name	SSN	Department	Employment Date	Hour	Rate	Gross		Large
4	b2437110	Mark	Spencer	450012432	Admin	1/22/2019	50	$75.00	$3,000.00		=LARGE(I:I,2)
5	b2437111	John	Bolt	341112434	Sales	7/24/2019	50	$44.30	$1,772.00		LARGE(array, k)
6	a2437112	James	Phrase	670022435	Sales	2/24/2018	52	$19.90	$835.00		
7	b2437113	Luther	Miles	882012539	Marketing	6/3/2017	58	$15.00	$1,770.00		
8	2437114	Harry	Cliton	553112632	Sales	12/28/2019	58	$55.50	$1,623.00		
9	2437115	Bells	Simpson	125512442	Personnel	1/5/2017	45	$12.00	$430.00		
10	b2437116	Bob	Kelly	522001248	Human Resource	8/23/2019	45	$12.00	$430.00		
11	b2437117	Martins	April	538012498	Sales	8/13/2018	58	$15.50	$1,807.00		
12	2437118	James	Kingsley	587012489	Admin	9/27/2018	58	$49.00	$1,960.00		
13	2437119	Robert	Hume	480026440	Sales	10/7/2019	30	$55.95	$1,808.00		
14	b2437120	Harold	Jason	552812450	Sales	8/30/2019	30	$45.20	$1,920		
15	b2437121	David	Kessington	421596508	Sales	2/11/2019	25	$33.16	$1,025.85		
16	b2437122	Davis	Gray	207843531	Marketing	3/27/2017	30	$32.64	$1,012.66		
17	a2437123	Benjamin	Samuel	317960683	Marketing	5/7/2018	25	$32.12	$999.47		
18	b2437124	Anderson	Smith	527728054	Sales	2/21/2018	45	$31.59	$986.28		
19	a2437125	Wright	Clark	200968363	Director	7/17/2017	29	$31.07	$973.09		
20	a2437126	Mitchell	Johnson	523191905	Procurement	5/14/2017	32	$30.54	$959.90		
21	a2437127	Thomas	Rodriguez	213597710	Sales	11/24/2016	45	$30.02	$946.71		
22	a2437128	Jackson	Perez	519214366	Marketing	12/9/2017	56	$29.50	$1,867.00		

It returns $3000 as the second-highest paid salary on the payroll.

	A	B	C	D	E	F	G	H	I	J	K
1						Midas Concept LLC					
2						Payroll					
3	Employee No	First Name	Last Name	SSN	Department	Employment Date	Hour	Rate	Gross		Large
4	b2437110	Mark	Spencer	450012432	Admin	1/22/2019	50	$75.00	$3,000.00		3000
5	b2437111	John	Bolt	341112434	Sales	7/24/2019	50	$44.30	$1,772.00		
6	a2437112	James	Phrase	670022435	Sales	2/24/2018	52	$19.90	$835.00		
7	b2437113	Luther	Miles	882012539	Marketing	6/3/2017	58	$15.00	$1,770.00		
8	2437114	Harry	Cliton	553112632	Sales	12/28/2019	58	$55.50	$1,623.00		
9	2437115	Bells	Simpson	125512442	Personnel	1/5/2017	45	$12.00	$430.00		
10	b2437116	Bob	Kelly	522001248	Human Resource	8/23/2019	45	$12.00	$430.00		
11	b2437117	Martins	April	538012498	Sales	8/13/2018	58	$15.50	$1,807.00		
12	2437118	James	Kingsley	587012489	Admin	9/27/2018	58	$49.00	$1,960.00		
13	2437119	Robert	Hume	480026440	Sales	10/7/2019	30	$55.95	$1,808.00		
14	b2437120	Harold	Jason	552812450	Sales	8/30/2019	30	$45.20	$1,920		
15	b2437121	David	Kessington	421596508	Sales	2/11/2019	25	$33.16	$1,025.85		
16	b2437122	Davis	Gray	207843531	Marketing	3/27/2017	30	$32.64	$1,012.66		
17	a2437123	Benjamin	Samuel	317960683	Marketing	5/7/2018	25	$32.12	$999.47		
18	b2437124	Anderson	Smith	527728054	Sales	2/21/2018	45	$31.59	$986.28		
19	a2437125	Wright	Clark	200968363	Director	7/17/2017	29	$31.07	$973.09		
20	a2437126	Mitchell	Johnson	523191905	Procurement	5/14/2017	32	$30.54	$959.90		
21	a2437127	Thomas	Rodriguez	213597710	Sales	11/24/2016	45	$30.02	$946.71		
22	a2437128	Jackson	Perez	519214366	Marketing	12/9/2017	56	$29.50	$1,867.00		

Small Function

The Excel Small Function is the direct opposite of the Large Function returns the Kth smallest value from the sample. The general syntax for the Small function is given thus;

=SMALL(Cell Array, K)

Let's use the SMALL function to find out the least paid Salary on the Midas Concept Payroll.

=SMALL(I:I,1)

	A	B	C	D	E	F	G	H	I	J	K
SUM				fx	=SMALL(I:I,2)						
1						Midas Concept LLC					
2						Payroll					
3	Employee No	First Name	Last Name	SSN	Department	Employment Date	Hour	Rate	Gross		Small
4	b2437110	Mark	Spencer	450012432	Admin	1/22/2019	50	$75.00	$3,000.00		=SMALL(I:I,2)
5	b2437111	John	Bolt	341112434	Sale	Returns the k-th smallest value in a data set. For example, the fifth smallest number				SMALL(array, k)	
6	a2437112	James	Phrase	670022435	Sales	2/24/2018	52	$19.90	$835.00		
7	b2437113	Luther	Miles	882012539	Marketing	6/3/2017	58	$15.00	$1,770.00		
8	2437114	Harry	Cliton	553112632	Sales	12/28/2019	58	$55.50	$1,623.00		
9	2437115	Bells	Simpson	125512442	Personnel	1/5/2017	45	$12.00	$430.00		
10	b2437116	Bob	Kelly	522001248	Human Resource	8/23/2019	45	$12.00	$430.00		
11	b2437117	Martins	April	538012498	Sales	8/13/2018	58	$15.50	$1,807.00		
12	2437118	James	Kingsley	587012489	Admin	9/27/2018	58	$49.00	$1,960.00		
13	2437119	Robert	Hume	480026440	Sales	10/7/2019	30	$55.95	$1,808.00		
14	b2437120	Harold	Jason	552812450	Sales	8/30/2019	30	$45.20	$1,920		
15	b2437121	David	Kessington	421596508	Sales	2/11/2019	25	$33.16	$1,025.85		
16	b2437122	Davis	Gray	207843531	Marketing	3/27/2017	30	$32.64	$1,012.66		
17	a2437123	Benjamin	Samuel	317960683	Marketing	5/7/2018	25	$32.12	$999.47		
18	b2437124	Anderson	Smith	527728054	Sales	2/21/2018	45	$31.59	$986.28		
19	a2437125	Wright	Clark	200968363	Director	7/17/2017	29	$31.07	$973.09		
20	a2437126	Mitchell	Johnson	523191905	Procurement	5/14/2017	32	$30.54	$959.90		
21	a2437127	Thomas	Rodriguez	213597710	Sales	11/24/2016	45	$30.02	$946.71		
22	a2437128	Jackson	Perez	519214366	Marketing	12/9/2017	56	$29.50	$1,867.00		

This returned $430 as our lowest salary paid.

Exercise: Carry out a SMALL function for the second least paid amount as Salary on the Midas Concept Payroll

CORREL Function

CORREL means Correlation. We can use the **CORRELATION Function** in Excel to find the correlation coefficient between two variables. Correlation Coefficient is used to find out how strong the relationship between two data. For instance, in our data below, we want to find out the relation between Math and Biology scores.

	L	M	N	O	P	Q
1						
2			Students	Maths	Biology	CORRELATION
3			1	43	99	
4			2	21	65	
5			3	25	80	
6			4	100	79	
7			5	42	75	
8			6	57	87	
9			7	59	81	
10			8	50	73	
11			9	89	82	

The formula always returns a value between -1 and 1. If the relationship between the data is between zero (0) to one (1), it indicates a strong positive relationship. A correlation coefficient of 1 means that for every positive increase in one variable, there is a positive increase of a fixed proportion in the other. So, it is a proper correlation. If the correlation coefficient is between minus one (-1) and zero (0), it indicates a strong negative relationship. It means that for every positive increase in one variable, there is a negative decrease of a fixed proportion in the other. For example, the amount of gas in the tank of a car decreases in perfect correlation with the speed of the vehicle.

If the result is zero (O), it indicates no relationship at all. It means for every increase; there is no positive or negative increase.

Let's look at the example below, where we have students and their scores in Math and Biology. We want to find out if there is any relationship at all

		Students	Maths	Biology	CORRELATION
		1	43	99	
		2	21	65	
		3	25	80	
		4	100	79	
		5	42	75	
		6	57	87	
		7	59	81	
		8	50	73	
		9	89	82	

We enter the correlation formula

=CORREL(O3:O11,P3:P11)

	O2		fx	Math		
		Students	Math	Biology	CORRELATION	
		1	43	99	0.212175931	
		2	21	65		
		3	25	80		
		4	100	79		
		5	42	75		
		6	57	87		
		7	59	81		
		8	50	73		
		9	89	82		

When we hit the ENTER Key, we have 0.21, which means there is a close relationship between Math and Biology. It means that improvement in Math scores will improve on Biology Score.

Chapter Nine
Charts in Excel

Charts

A chart is a powerful tool that allows you to display data in a variety of different visual formats. To use charts effectively in Excel, you need to understand how various charts are created. We will be looking at several Excel Charts in this chapter. They include Bar Charts, Column Charts, Pie Charts, Line Charts, Area Charts, Doughnut, Scatter Charts, Surface Charts, and Radar Charts.

Column Chart

Column Charts use vertical bars to represent data. They can be used with different data types, but they are more commonly used when comparing two or more data. Let's illustrate this with our sales data for different cities for two years. The sales data is in millions.

	A	B	C	D	E
1			Sales Data		
2		Cities	2018	2019	
3		San Antonio	65	70	
4		New York	55	65	
5		Dallas	45	52	
6		San Jose	41	42	
7		Chicago	45	41	
8		Fort Worth	32	23	
9		Seattle	40	25	
10		Denver	50	24	
11		Boston	39	19	
12		Memphis	36	60	
13					

To convert this data to a column chart,

- Select the entire data

B3		▼	fx	San Antonio	
	A	B	C	D	E
1			Sales Data		
2		Cities	2018	2019	
3		San Antonio	65	70	
4		New York	55	65	
5		Dallas	45	52	
6		San Jose	41	42	
7		Chicago	45	41	
8		Fort Worth	32	23	
9		Seattle	40	25	
10		Denver	50	24	
11		Boston	39	19	
12		Memphis	36	60	

- Click on the 'Insert' tab
- There are different Column chart options - 2D column, 2D Bar, 3D bar, Cone, Cylinder, pyramid, etc
- Click on any of the column charts that better represents your data.

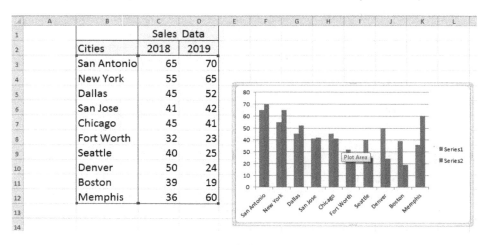

Next, you can edit the entire Chart by selecting it and clicking on the "Layout" tab. Here you can edit the title of the Chart e.g., change ours to "Sales Data" and edit the chart Legend. (Change the Series1 and Series2 to 2018 and 2019 respectively). You can also remove gridlines, customize Axis title, legend, data labels, data table, Axes plot area, etc. from the "Layout" tab.

Cities	Sales Data	
	2018	2019
San Antonio	65	70
New York	55	65
Dallas	45	52
San Jose	41	42
Chicago	45	41
Fort Worth	32	23
Seattle	40	25
Denver	50	24
Boston	39	19
Memphis	36	60

Line Charts

Line Charts are ideal for showing trends. For example, let's look at the data below, showing the temperature of Chicago for the past seven days.

Temperature for Chicago For the Past seven Days		
Day	Temperature (Fahrenheit)	
Monday	43	
Tueday	53	
Wednesday	50	
Thursday	57	
Friday	59	
Saturday	67	
Sunday	75	

We can represent the above data as a line chart by highlighting the entire data > click on the "Insert" tab and under the 'Chart' group select 'Line.' You can select between 2D or 3D line charts. Other types of line charts include – stacked line chart, line charts with markers, and a stacked line chart with markers.

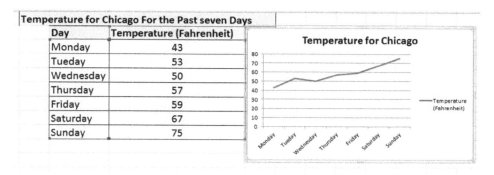

Temperature for Chicago For the Past seven Days	
Day	Temperature (Fahrenheit)
Monday	43
Tueday	53
Wednesday	50
Thursday	57
Friday	59
Saturday	67
Sunday	75

Below is a stacked chart with markers used in representing our data.

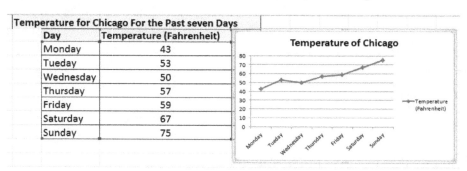

Temperature for Chicago For the Past seven Days	
Day	Temperature (Fahrenheit)
Monday	43
Tueday	53
Wednesday	50
Thursday	57
Friday	59
Saturday	67
Sunday	75

Pie Chart

Pie Charts are generally used to show percentage or proportional data, and usually, the percentage represented by each category is provided next to the corresponding slice of pie. Pie charts are suitable for comparing data with six (6) categories or less. Pie charts are a popular way to show how individual figures (e.g., quarterly sales figures) contribute to a total figure (e.g., annual sales, etc.).Pie Chart makes it easy to compare data according to their proportion. Each value is shown as a slice of a pie. We have two significant types of pie charts – 2D and 3D

215

pie charts. Other examples of pie charts include Exploded Pie Chart, Pie of Pie, Bar of Pie, and Exploded Pie in 3D.

Let's illustrate the Pie Charts using the Temperature for Chicago data.

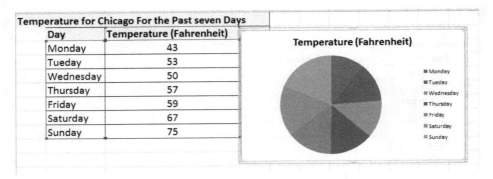

We can also represent the same data as an Exploded pie chart.

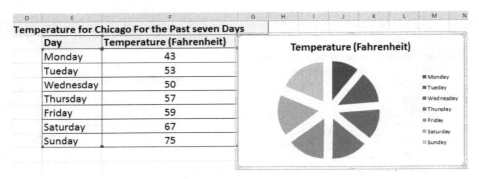

Below is what we get when we represent our data as a Pie of Pie chart.

Temperature for Chicago For the Past seven Days	
Day	Temperature (Fahrenheit)
Monday	43
Tueday	53
Wednesday	50
Thursday	57
Friday	59
Saturday	67
Sunday	75

Finally, for Pie of Bar Chart, we get

Temperature for Chicago For the Past seven Days	
Day	Temperature (Fahrenheit)
Monday	43
Tueday	53
Wednesday	50
Thursday	57
Friday	59
Saturday	67
Sunday	75

Temperature (Fahrenheit)

■ Monday
■ Tueday
■ Wednesday
■ Thursday
■ Friday
■ Saturday
■ Sunday

Bar Chart

Bar Chart is like the column chart, but in bar charts, we use the horizontal bars instead of vertical bars in the column chart. A bar chart is useful when the text representing each data item is extended. For example,

	Boys	Girls
No of out of school children in Africa	40%	40%
No of Out of school children in Asia	9%	9%
No of Out of School Children in Middle East	29%	39%

If we were to represent the above data using a column chart, the title for each data item would be too long to display vertically. So we use a bar chart to represent the above data.

A	B	C
	Boys	Girls
No of out of school children in Africa	40%	40%
No of Out of school children in Asia	9%	9%
No of Out of School Children in Middle East	29%	39%

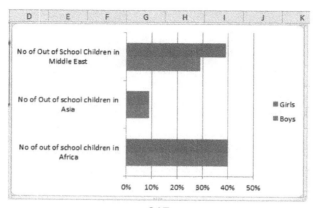

There are several types of bar charts - 2D, 3D, clustered, stacked, clustered horizontal cylinder, stacked horizontal cylinder, clustered horizontal cone, stacked horizontal cone, clustered horizontal pyramid, and stacked horizontal pyramid.

Surface Chart

A surface chart is useful when you want to find out the optimal combination between two sets of data. We have different Surface charts - 3D surface chart, wireframe 3D surface chart, Contour surface chart, and wireframe contour surface chart.

Let's look at our data below.

	Financial	Marketing	Effort
Recruit	346	110	160
Environment	406	504	46
Assets	193	305	454
Buildings	230	460	597
Expenses	330	520	404

We can represent the above data using Surface charts. Below is a depiction of our data in a 3D surface chart.

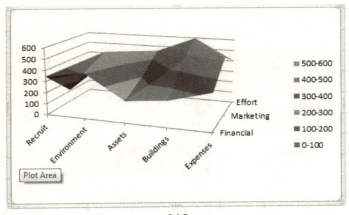

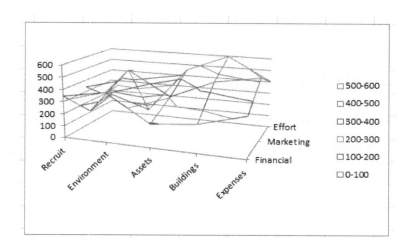

Wireframe Surface chart

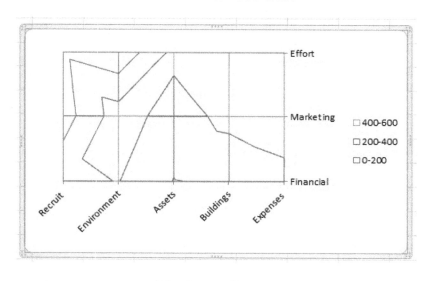

Wireframe Contour

Recommended chart

This is a feature that allows Excel to suggest several ideal charts that suits your kind of data. In order to use the recommended chart option in Excel, select data in your worksheet > go to the "Insert" tab and click on "Recommended Charts." This provides a customized set of charts that are recommended by Excel.

219

Pivot Table

A Pivot table is a tool that allows users to reorganize and summarize selected columns and rows of data in a spreadsheet or database table to obtain a desired report. The Pivot table doesn't change the spreadsheet or database itself but adds a new worksheet with a summary report.

To illustrate how the Pivot tables work, we will use our Midas Concept LLC Payroll spreadsheet shown below for this illustration.

	O1	▾	f_x					
	A	B	C	D	E	F	G	H	I
1						**Midas Concept LLC**			
2						**Payroll**			
3	**Employee No**	**First Name**	**Last Name**	**SSN**	**Department**	**Employment Date**	**Hour**	**Rate**	**Gross**
4	b2437110	Mark	Spencer	450012432	Admin	1/22/2019	50	$75.00	$3,000.00
5	b2437111	John	Bolt	341112434	Sales	7/24/2019	50	$44.30	$1,772.00
6	a2437112	James	Phrase	670022435	Sales	2/24/2018	52	$19.90	$835.00
7	b2437113	Luther	Miles	882012539	Marketing	6/3/2017	58	$15.00	$1,770.00
8	2437114	Harry	Cliton	553112632	Sales	12/28/2019	58	$55.50	$1,623.00
9	2437115	Bells	Simpson	125512442	Personnel	1/5/2017	45	$12.00	$430.00
10	b2437116	Bob	Kelly	522001248	Human Resource	8/23/2019	45	$12.00	$430.00
11	b2437117	Martins	April	538012498	Sales	8/13/2018	58	$15.50	$1,807.00
12	2437118	James	Kingsley	587012489	Admin	9/27/2018	58	$49.00	$1,960.00
13	2437119	Robert	Hume	480026440	Sales	10/7/2019	30	$55.95	$1,808.00
14	b2437120	Harold	Jason	552812450	Sales	8/30/2019	30	$45.20	$1,920
15	b2437121	David	Kessington	421596508	Sales	2/11/2019	25	$33.16	$1,025.85
16	b2437122	Davis	Gray	207843531	Marketing	3/27/2017	30	$32.64	$1,012.66
17	a2437123	Benjamin	Samuel	317960683	Marketing	5/7/2018	25	$32.12	$999.47
18	b2437124	Anderson	Smith	527728054	Sales	2/21/2018	45	$31.59	$986.28
19	a2437125	Wright	Clark	200968363	Director	7/17/2017	29	$31.07	$973.09
20	a2437126	Mitchell	Johnson	523191905	Procurement	5/14/2017	32	$30.54	$959.90
21	a2437127	Thomas	Rodriguez	213597710	Sales	11/24/2016	45	$30.02	$946.71
22	a2437128	Jackson	Perez	519214366	Marketing	12/9/2017	56	$29.50	$1,867.00

To create a pivot table to show the departments and their salaries.
- We need to go to the database for which we need to create a pivot table
- Click on the "Insert" tab and click on the Pivot table from the 'tables group.'

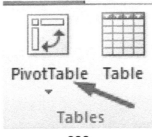

- A "Create PivotTable" window pops up as shown below;

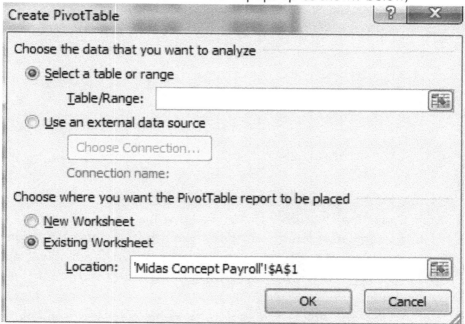

- From this window, select the cell range from which the Pivot table should be created. In other words, select the entire data required for the Pivot table creation, you could as well select the entire table if you want the pivot table to cover your entire table.

- Next, select either New Sheet or Existing sheet. If we choose "New Sheet" and click 'OK,' it will automatically create a new sheet in the existing workbook, and the pivot table will be placed on that new sheet. However, if we click on the "Existing Worksheet," we have to give a new location. That means we will select a cell within an existing sheet to place the pivot table. You can select the location from any of your current worksheets. For our illustration, we will choose 'New Worksheet' and click on the OK button. This creates a new Excel sheet, just before your current Excel sheet. Once the Excel sheet is created, you will find the pivot table result on a blank space with the Pivot table number and on the right-hand side the PivotTable Fields.

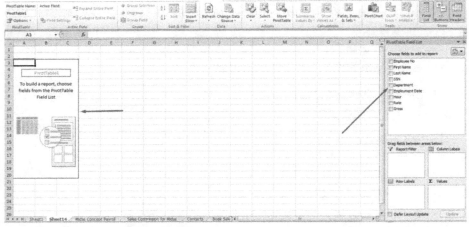

- Under the PivotTable Fields, we have the selected headings on our database listed, e.g., Employee no, First name, Last name, etc. On our PivotTable window beneath the PivotTable Fields, we have Filters, Columns, Rows, and Values.

- <u>Values:</u> The Values box is a large rectangular box beneath the columns heading. It calculates and counts data. For instance, if we click and drag the Gross field from the PivotTable Fields to the 'Values' box, it will automatically give us the sum of the Gross salaries.

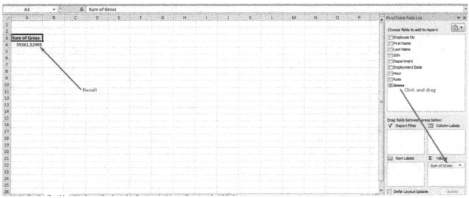

We can change the value field setting from "Sum" to other calculations by clicking on the drop-down arrow on the field you dragged to the Values box and click on "Value Field Settings."

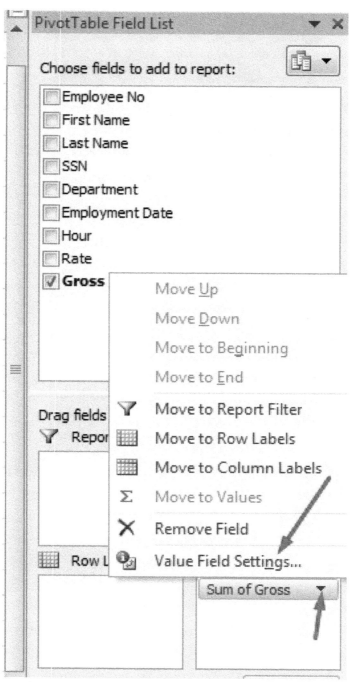

A pop-up window opens.

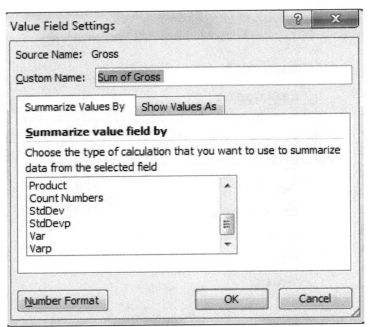

You could see that "Sum" is the default calculation. You can change this default calculation to any function e.g., Count, Average, Max, Min, Product, Count Numbers, StdDev, StdDVp, Var, etc. This way, when a data Field item is dragged to the 'Values' box, it produces the result of the selected calculation.

Rows: Placing a data field in the row area displays the unique value from that field down the rows on the left side of the PivotTable. For instance, if we drag the data field for the "Employee Department" to the Rows, it displays the content of that row once and sums their salaries.

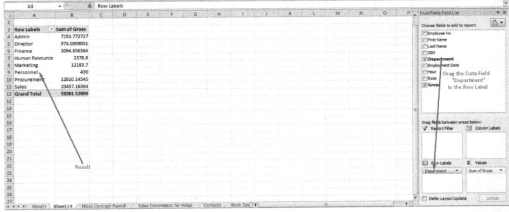

What this means is that for example, Sales comes more than once in our database, but the PivotTable will group all the Sales into one cell and give the sum of all the salaries of employees in the Sales department. The same goes for Admin, Marketing, Human Resource, etc. Below is how your database will look if you put the data field in the rows label area.

	A3	f_x Row Labels

	A	B
3	**Row Labels** ▾	**Sum of Gross**
4	Admin	7153.772727
5	Director	973.0909091
6	Finance	3094.856364
7	Human Resource	2378.8
8	Marketing	12183.7
9	Personnel	430
10	Procurement	12610.14545
11	Sales	20437.16364
12	**Grand Total**	59261.52909
13		Sum of Gross
		Value: 59261.52909
		Row: Grand Total
14		

Column Labels: The column area comprises of headings that stretches across the top of the column. For instance, if we drag the hour data field into the column area, it displays the content of the data field horizontally and shows the sum at the end.

Filter: Filter is an optional set of one or more drop-down lists at the top of the pivot table. For instance, if we drag the employment Data field into the Filter area, it will add the Employment date column on the left from a drop-down menu allowing you to select which 'Employment date' data you want to be displayed.

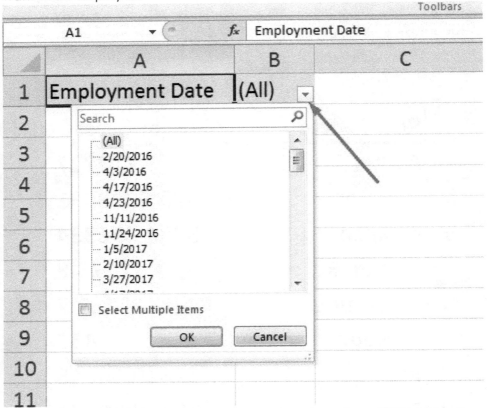

If we want the data for an employee employed on the 4/17/2016, when we click on that date on the PivotTable, it displays the details. The filter allows us to apply filters to the PivotTable easily.

APPENDIX 1

Microsoft Excel Keyboard Shortcut Keys

F2	Edit the Selected Cell	F5	Go to a specific Cell
F7	Spell check selected text and/or document	F11	Create chart
Ctrl + Shift + ;	Enter the current time	Ctrl + ;	Enter the current date
Alt+ Shift+ F1	Insert New Worksheet	Shift + F3	Open the Excel formula Window
Shift + F5	Bring up search box	Ctrl + A	Select all contents of worksheet
Ctrl + B	Bold highlighted selection	Ctrl + I	Italicize highlighted selection
Ctrl + C	Copy selected text	Ctrl + V	Paste
Ctrl + D	Fill	Ctrl + K	Insert hyperlink
Ctrl + F	Open find and replace options	Ctrl + G	Open go-to options
Ctrl + H	Open find and replace options	Ctrl + U	Underline highlighted selection
Ctrl + 0	Hide column	Ctrl + 5	Strikethrough highlighted selection
Ctrl + O	Open options	Ctrl + N	Open new document
Ctrl + P	Open Print dialog box	Ctrl + S	Save
Ctrl + Z	Undo last action	Ctrl + F9	Minimize current window
Ctrl + F10	Maximize currently selected window	Ctrl + F6	Switch between open workbooks/ windows
Ctrl + X	Cut	Ctrl + W	Close Window
Ctrl + T	Create table	Ctrl + U	Underline
Ctrl + 1	Format Box	Ctrl + 9	Hide row
Ctrl + Y	Repeat	Shift + Ctrl + 9	Unhide row
Shift + Ctrl	Unhide Column	Ctrl + ~	Show

			formulas/values
+ O			
Ctrl + '	Copy above formula	Ctrl + [	Precedent
Ctrl +]	Dependents	Ctrl + Space	Select Column
Ctrl + Enter	Fill selection with entry	Ctrl + F2	Print Preview
Alt + W + F + F	Freeze Pane	Alt	Activate Menu Bar
Shift + Space	Select Row	Ctrl + =	Add Row
Shift + Alt + →	Group Selected Row/Columns	Shift + Alt + ←	Ungroup Selected Rows/Columns
Alt + E + S	Open Paste special Menu	Alt + E + S + F	Paste only formulas
Alt + E + S + V	Paste only values	Alt + E + S + T	Paste only formats
Shift + F2	Insert a Cell Comment	Ctrl + Shift + 7	Add outline cell border
Ctrl + Shift + -	Remove Cell Border	Alt + H + O + M	Copy or move a worksheet
Alt + H + O + R	Rename a worksheet	Alt + H + O	Increase decimal
Alt + H + 9	Decrease Decimal	Shift + Ctrl + #	Date Format
Shift + Ctrl + $	Dollar Format	Shift + Ctrl + %	Percentage Format
Alt + =	Sum Function	F12	Displays the Save As dialogue box
F11	Creates a chart of the data in the current range in a separate chartsheet	Shift + F9	Calculate the current worksheet
Alt + F4	Closes Microsoft Excel	Ctrl + F1	Displays or Hides Ribbon
Ctrl + Home	Go to Cell A1	Ctrl + End	Go to the Last Cell of the table

APPENDIX 2

	Employee No	First Name	Last Name	SSN	Department	Employment Date	Hour	Rate	Gross
					Midas Concept LLC				
					Payroll				
4	b2437110	Mark	Spencer	450012432	Admin	1/22/2019	50	$75.00	$3,000.00
5	b2437111	John	Bolt	341112434	Sales	7/24/2019	50	$44.30	$1,772.00
6	a2437112	James	Phrase	670022435	Sales	2/24/2018	52	$19.90	$835.00
7	b2437113	Luther	Miles	882012539	Marketing	6/3/2017	58	$15.00	$1,770.00
8	2437114	Harry	Cliton	553112632	Sales	12/28/2019	58	$55.50	$1,623.00
9	2437115	Bells	Simpson	125512442	Personnel	1/5/2017	45	$12.00	$430.00
10	b2437116	Bob	Kelly	522001248	Human Resource	8/23/2019	45	$12.00	$430.00
11	b2437117	Martins	April	538012498	Sales	8/13/2018	58	$15.50	$1,807.00
12	2437118	James	Kingsley	587012489	Admin	9/27/2018	58	$49.00	$1,960.00
13	2437119	Robert	Hume	480026440	Sales	10/7/2019	30	$55.95	$1,808.00
14	b2437120	Harold	Jason	552812450	Sales	8/30/2019	30	$45.20	$1,920
15	b2437121	David	Kessington	421596508	Sales	2/11/2019	25	$33.16	$1,025.85
16	b2437122	Davis	Gray	207843531	Marketing	3/27/2017	30	$32.64	$1,012.66
17	a2437123	Benjamin	Samuel	317960683	Marketing	5/7/2018	25	$32.12	$999.47
18	b2437124	Anderson	Smith	527728054	Sales	2/21/2018	45	$31.59	$986.28
19	a2437125	Wright	Clark	200968363	Director	7/17/2017	29	$31.07	$973.09
20	a2437126	Mitchell	Johnson	523191905	Procurement	5/14/2017	32	$30.54	$959.90
21	a2437127	Thomas	Rodriguez	213597710	Sales	11/24/2016	45	$30.02	$946.71
22	a2437128	Jackson	Perez	519214366	Marketing	12/9/2017	56	$29.50	$1,867.00
23	a2437129	Lewis	Hill	337946786	Finance	3/24/2019	40	$28.97	$1,270.00
24	a2437130	Robert	Jones	200824449	Sales	4/3/2016	35	$28.45	$907.14
25	b2437131	White	Turner	445549853	Procurement	8/26/2017	25	$27.93	$894
26	a2437132	Harris	Brown	420188090	Marketing	9/25/2019	24	$27.40	$880.75
27	a2437133	Philip	Walker	300302563	Marketing	2/20/2016	17	$26.88	$867.56
28	b2437134	Davis	Green	518634252	Sales	3/26/2018	45	$26.36	$854.37
29	b2437135	Martins	Hall	576571427	Procurement	4/17/2016	45	$25.83	$9,562.00
30	b2437136	Adams	Campbell	311927852	Admin	9/10/2019	37	$25.31	$827.99
31	a2437137	Allen	Millwe	400681788	Human Resource	7/8/2017	28	$24.78	$814.80
32	b2437138	Garcia	Parker	504096781	Sales	7/23/2019	39	$24.26	$801.61
33	a2437139	Young	Gonzalez	479068639	Sales	10/16/2017	45	$23.74	$788.42
34	a2437140	Evans	Moore	518875263	Sales	11/10/2018	35	$23.21	$775.23
35	b2437141	Edward	Martinez	442421302	Marketing	11/24/2019	25	$22.69	$762.04
36	b2437142	Carter	Collins	254401633	Admin	2/10/2017	35	$22.17	$749
37	a2437143	Robison	King	500604265	Finance	4/23/2016	33	$21.64	$735.65
38	a2437144	Ronald	Christopher	576952245	Sales	5/12/2018	40	$21.12	$722.46
39	b2437145	John	Richard	678123891	Marketing	5/20/2019	32	$20.60	$709.27
40	b2437146	Anothony	Robert	426680168	Human Resource	4/17/2017	32	$20.07	$1,134.00
41	a2437147	Charles	Steven	518823644	Sales	7/29/2018	32	$19.55	$1,132.00
42	a2437148	Mark	Edward	328266494	Marketing	8/3/2017	58	$19.02	$669.70
43	a2437149	Donald	William	488985763	Marketing	8/10/2019	58	$18.50	$656.51
44	a2437150	Brian	Jeff	440343893	Marketing	11/11/2016	35	$17.98	$643.32
45	a2437151	Sandra	Richard	346865540	Sales	6/15/2019	20	$17.45	$630.13
46	b2437152	Jennifer	Kenneth	300802552	Admin	6/18/2019	24	$16.93	$616.94
47	b2437153	Lisa	Robert	260776719	Procurement	10/20/2018	32	$16.41	$603.75
48	b2437154	Patricia	George	221383153	Procurement	4/20/2018	51	$15.88	$590.55
49	a2437155	Maria	Charles	574465023	Sales	6/2/2019	30	$15.36	$577.36
50	a2437156	Nancy	Kevin	108524328	Marketing	8/24/2019	22	$14.84	$834.00
51	a2437157	Donna	Joseph	169105949	Finance	9/7/2019	22	$14.31	$550.98

52	a2437158	Susan	Mark	516220026	Finance	3/26/2019	34	$13.79	$538
53	b2437159	Barbara	Donald	503297341	Sales	7/27/2019	36	$13.26	$524.60
54	a2437160	Kimberly	Gonzalez	687102257	Marketing	12/28/2019	40	$12.74	$511.41

About the Author

Derrick Richard is a tech geek with several years of experience in the ICT industry. He passionately follows latest tech trends and his passion is in figuring out the solution to complex problems.

Derrick holds a Bachelor and a Master's Degree in ICT respectively from Georgetown University, Washington DC. He lives in Sarasota, Florida.